About the Author

I am a devoted Christian, and I have been serving the Lord for the past twelve years. I have been blessed with a loving husband, and I can proudly state that he is my soulmate, predestined to support me through the difficulty of sickness. We have two amazing daughters, and our family continues to remain rooted in our faith.

From Ashes to Beauty

Amanda Short

From Ashes to Beauty

Olympia Publishers
London

www.olympiapublishers.com

OLYMPIA PAPERBACK EDITION

A CIP catalogue record for this title is
available from the British Library.

ISBN: 978-1-80074-471-4

First Published in 2022

Olympia Publishers
Tallis House
2 Tallis Street
London
EC4Y 0AB

Printed in Great Britain

Dedication

I dedicate this book to my husband, Rory, my two amazing daughters, Nicola and Michelle, as well as to my late mother, Maria, as she played an enormous role from where I found this inspiration. I know that she rejoices from heaven, cheering me on to new heights.

Acknowledgements

I have found that having an idea and turning it into a book is as hard as it sounds, and this experience was both internally challenging but at the same time rewarding. The impact of this book in my own spiritual journey has been beyond my expectation, and more than I could have ever imagined. None of this would be possible without the unwavering support of my God, as He stood by me with every struggle, but most importantly through bringing a more in-depth revelation of the perfect relationship He has to offer. He knew before the beginning of time how my dream to see the elevation of worship and celebration could result in a sure example of how rewarding a product of hard work is. My Lord of Lights ensured that I could develop this interactive relationship into sustaining my troubled heart when I ran away from my hiding place of redemption.

Opening up my heart in the most fragile season of my life, has given me the satisfaction and vision that the sharing of my testimony of healing can be a surreal process. In impacting those people around me, into restoring their spirit into one of devotion, I have found a renewed sense of awe and wonder of how marvellous His love for me is. I want to give God all the glory as I strived to grow and help others grow. I have spent many hours crafting prayers in the conclusion of each topic and know that because of this I can boldly declare that moments spent in this brought the gentle guidance of Him to manifest in my spiritual journey.

I am forever indebted to Kristina Smith, my production co-ordinator at Olympia Publishers, for her ongoing support, dedication to give me guidance as this is my first experience as a writer, as well as her patience during every step of the way, and for walking the road beside me through all the necessary processes to bring my vision to life. I also want to thank them for seeing something in me and recognised the value I could bring to other believers. I can honestly say that their expertise brought a broader understanding of how intricate the publishing world is, and it is because of their efforts and encouragements that I have a legacy to pass on to my family.

To my dear friend, Karin, thank you that you have been a true example of how a devoted and humble servant of God looks like, and your supernatural ability to know which area of my life I need prayer in, and these revelations were included where these crafted prayer by the Holy Spirit applied to these topics

To my dear friend, Trudi, words cannot express my gratitude that you took time out from your busy schedule to proofread, and provide valid revisions, that ensured that my book is ready to be sent into the realm of the publishing world.

Last but not least, to my family, Rory, my closest confidant as well as being my cheerleader, Nicci, my proof-reader with the quickest turnaround time I could hope for, as well as making my eyes open to see the value this work of inspiration could be, and Michelle, my prayer warrior and daughter of our living God, as well as her willingness to lend her ear when I was eager to see the next stage of production come to fruition.

I can boldly confess that they were as important in making this book a success, as my faith and trust level that stems from the close relationship that I have been blessed by.

I believe that I am true evidence that as His gentle whisper of restoration upheld me, the surrendering of my heart to make a difference into the spiritual journey of my fellow believers, could be a shout of victory.

INTRODUCTION

The purpose of this work of inspiration stems from a road of redemption and healing that the Lord has been leading me into, and He has faithfully taken me on a journey from ashes to beauty.

The background to the road I was on is based on spending a holiday with loved ones after two months of a grueling chemotherapy road and the message of the Christmas morning's sermon, focused on "Making a difference".

The Lord spoke so loud and clear that I must focus on the testimony of my healing, and this is the main reason for creating a work of inspiration. I felt led by the Holy Spirit to respond to place His Kingdom as my utmost priority, to support those that need some encouragement to also walk the road to recovery, with victory and overcoming one's circumstances as the ultimate prize. A few months passed by where I found myself in a place of living life without believing I could achieve success, where my destiny was meant to be touching people's lives, expanding His Kingdom.

The impact I first believed I could achieve did not seem real, so I did what we sometimes do, where we fail to understand the influence our dreams of being obedient to Him can bring about. But this is the time to be bold and place the worth of my gift and the dream He placed years ago in my heart and soul, to be shared amongst anyone needing to hear His whisper of grace and mercy, guiding us onto a road of healing and restoration. I was led to a profound realisation that the Lord does not want your ability but your availability.

I would like to share the scripture that spoke to my heart, that inspired me to share the broken pieces that were made whole by surrendering my all to Him, with the following scripture:

Psalm 1:3

"He is like a tree planted beside streams of water that bears fruit in season and whose leaf does not wither. Whatever he does prosper."

This revelation brought me under His loving embrace, ensuring that I could experience His peace and mercy as a daughter of the only Living God. This was also the "wake up call" that drew me into His Kingdom. I was crying out in hunger to find a place of comfort and peace that caused all understanding of Christianity to become clear beyond doubt.

He knows in what stage or season we are in, and sometimes God's calling and moulding of your character can take a lifetime, but if we surrender all our dreams and hopes to Him, He enables us to endure the moulding and shaping of our lives. There is no other fact that remains but to give my most in serving and making a change in His kingdom!

I pray the revelation that the following scripture brought me before His throne room over my day will do the same for you:

1 Chronicles 16:29.

"Give to the Lord the glory He deserves! Bring your offering and come into His presence. Worship the Lord in all His holy splendour."

I pray that you will stay blessed and rejoice in the knowledge of how Great our God is! Worship Him in spirit and truth, being rooted in the holiness that the Lord reveals with abundance.

THE JOURNEY

<u>Staying true to His word</u>
I have realized that striving to have every area of your life exactly like you wish it to be can never be accomplished if you are not completely honest with yourself. Priorities and setting Jesus at the centre of all you think, do, and hope for are a sure recipe of creating a sense of belonging, bringing glory to His name.

I have found that trying to compare your path in your spiritual walk with your peers and family members is not from God and can never truly ensure that a devoted frame of mind aligns with your destiny. Great is the knowledge that nothing is impossible with our God. After all, He has never placed any words of judgement over us.

Fear of failure and the weight we place on our own shoulders should never be the driving force behind having an excuse in chasing your dreams. Add into the process of surrendering and making "God choices", I can only testify that the confident surrendering to Him has made an impact in my life and my outlook on my future. I have made a commitment to walking in truth, accepting and acknowledging His love and guidance, steering me towards my salvation.

I believe that to do this is for me to make a conscious decision every day to stop living in neutral mode or in apology of my past mistakes or misconceptions of what makes me perfect. In saying this, I have experienced a loss of completeness, and I can only blame the deviation of my path towards refraining from proclaiming His hand in my life is due to being caught up in the material things of this world. But if I am honest with myself, this should not steal my time away from the all-consuming fire to share the inspiration and wonder that the Holy Spirit brings.

My prayer that refreshes my soul is:

Romans 8:31

"What shall we say about such things as these? If God is for us, who can ever be against us?"

My prayer being, "I am in a place of acknowledgement that I am in desperate need for Your hand in every season I walk through. I praise Your name, because if You are behind me and fighting my battles, who can steal my salvation away? Whatever the cost, I will continue to praise You and proclaim Your divine intervention in my victory and salvation. Amen."

A heart after Him

I am thankful that the level of my faith and trust in the complete assurance that my heart is secured in the Lord's hands is evident in all areas of my life. Specifically, in the valley and mountains in every season. What a wonderful joy it brings to me once I have given these areas over to Him, without expecting any judgement, knowing that His way is right, and all He asks from us is to lay our burdens at His feet, strengthening our spirit on a continuous basis.

I trust that His unconditional, everlasting love will be known in my innermost thoughts and that He knows the appropriate words in my prayer before I even realize it, giving me all the desires of my heart.

Today, I pray the following scripture over all His children, that we will continue to praise Him daily:

Proverbs 21:2

"People may be right in their own eyes, but the Lord examines their heart."

Thank You, Lord, that my heart can relate to the constant whisper that to enlarge my faith in You, You long for me to dwell under the covering of Your wings. There will be an end to any troubles I hide away from. You examine my heart, and You are pleased with the journey that I have travelled, because my eyes are fixed on the glorious work of the cross.

Reassurance of my faith

My last entry focused on trusting that my faith in experiencing His everlasting love will be known in my innermost thoughts, and still He constantly reassures me that I can be bold in drawing close to Him in my prayers, ensuring that all my fears are taken care of. The word is clear on us taking comfort that each day is new with abundant mercies, as well assuring us that we should not concern ourselves with what tomorrow holds. There can be seasons of thinking that Satan knows how to steal, kill, and destroy our faith, and the fear that the Lord will abandon us in the hour of need. But what a comfort it is that we are not condemned for our sins, but that we are born again by the Holy Spirit. From that moment on, there are no words to describe the revelation that any desperation I have felt is being lifted to Heaven.

The scripture on my heart today is:

Habakkuk 2:14.

"For the earth will be filled with the knowledge of the Lord's glory, as the waters cover the sea."

Today, my prayer is that the Lord will give me the power

of inner strength so that my entire life will be built on the love that flows from Him. Thank you, Lord, that I can conquer everything through You, and that You see every tear that we shed, considering those difficulties we endure but are afraid of giving over to You. Thank you that you listen to my prayer from the ends of the earth, where I call to You. When my heart is faint, You reassure me of Your grace and mercy.

FAITH

Rooted in faith

Today the scripture on my heart is:

Ephesians 2:10

"For we are God's workmanship, created in Christ Jesus to do good works, which God prepared in advance for us to do."

I am rooted in the knowledge that I have been created in Your image. There are no limits to Your handy work in my life; all You ask of me is to have faith in the blessings that You have designed for me. I will strive to continue to be in a place of doing good works. I will not, in return, seek anyone's approval of my actions but trust that You will guide me towards situations that require holding someone's head up and relying on the power of prayer and a supporting ear.

I pray that the following scripture will link to my prayers today:

Jeremiah 1:8–9

"'Do not be afraid of them, for I am with you and will rescue you,' declares the Lord. Then the Lord reached out His hand and touched my mouth and said to me, "'I have put my words in your mouth.'"

I pray that I will continue to be thankful, because I know that I was formed by Your hand, dreamed up in Your heart and placed in this world for a purpose.

My prayer today is that I will depend on Your prompting that this is a time in my current season where I need to refrain from setting limits to what You can do. I pray that I will not be distracted by the things of this world. I receive Your guidance and will continue to praise Your name because You are enough, and that I am worthy of Your grace, love, and mercy.

My heart rejoices

Today the scripture on my heart is the following:

Philippians 4:6

"Don't worry about anything, but instead pray about everything. Tell God what you need and thank Him for all He has done for you."

You draw me closer, and my heart rejoices in this. You raise me up, and I stand in amazement that there is no name above Your Name. I wait in Your presence and rely on the word that encourages me to be still and know that You are God. I will never fail to express the victory I have found in Your loving embrace. My heart belongs to You only, Lord. My devotion is Yours only. Seeing Your hand in my journey brings a lifechanging understanding to my spiritual eyes.

I will continue to speak truth into every season. All glory to You, Abba Father. I believe that the righteous Kingdom is announced in my faith-filled, blessed times of worship. I will not be in a place of feeling out of control, because I am under the covering of Your wings. Only You can satisfy my hunger to worship and rejoice in heaven's grace; thank You that the pressure is off me to perform, that I can always find a resting place in You, My Savior.

My prayer today is that the following scripture will be an echo

that will continue to support my level of faith in You:
1 Thessalonians 5:16–18
"Always be joyful. Never stop praying. Be thankful in all circumstances, for this is God's will for you who belong to Christ Jesus."

I pray that You will continue to be my rock of Peace. You alone are all that I need, as I stand on victory's solid foundation. Lord, I stand in awe of your work of righteousness that will place me before your throne of peace. I want to continue to dwell here, running towards my redemption, proclaiming to the heavens above that Your glory outshines any seasons of darkness and incompleteness.

Foundation of faith

Today the scripture on my heart is the following:
Timothy 3:16–17
"All scripture is inspired by God and is useful to teach us what is true and to make us realize what is wrong in our lives. It corrects us when we are wrong and teaches us to do what is right. God uses it to prepare and equip his people to do good works."

The prompting by the Holy Spirit today reminds me of this scripture, that my inspiration comes by obeying Our Prince of Peace and by spending time in the Word. Striving to use His guidance that will surely prepare and equip me, especially for my daily walk through every valley, is a priority that draws me closer to defeating my enemies.

I choose to remain a faithful servant and be Kingdom-focused in an effort to make a difference in a small way. I believe by doing this I can show His grace and mercy throughout my interaction with others, exposing the peace that comes when my foundation in my faith is rooted in His grace. My experience is that I can have the boldness to enter His throne room because I can be bold in declaring the freedom that stems from sitting at the feet of Jesus. I can have faith that He will deal with all my needs for any specific situation on my heart. We do not have to feel that our difficulties are impossible to be conquered. He never expects me to do this without His guidance and reminders of His promises.

There is no doubt that I need to trust that my innermost thoughts are already known to Him, that my unspoken desires will be taken care of.

I pray the following scripture:

Romans 3:23–24

"For everyone has sinned; we all fall short of God's glorious standard. Yet God, in His grace, freely makes us right in His sight. He did this through Christ Jesus when He freed us from the penalty of sin."

My prayer is that I will have the ability to continue to let Him move my heart, saturated with His grace and righteousness. Let me be able to fully trust Him and know that every situation has been dealt with, and that His perfect timing means that I can stand secure in the knowledge that His glorious light will guide my path forward. I rely on the fact that there is a constant stream of water that brings about a time of restoration, ensuring security in my daily walk with Him.

He will fulfill His promises of a storehouse of salvation, wisdom, and knowledge. I will praise Your name because You have used my sufferings to build my faith. Let my faith increase at a speed that I cannot imagine, and my heart is thankful for this. Let me remain under Your covering and let Your inspiration fill me with a renewed sense of peace.

STRENGTH

<u>Being complete in Him</u>

Today I am reminded of the scripture that raises my awareness of His strength:

Psalm 46:1–3

"God is our refuge and strength, an ever-present help in trouble. Therefore, we will not fear, though the earth give way and the mountains fall into the heart of the sea, though its waters roar and foam and the mountains quake with their surging."

Living life with joy in your heart is a gift that can impact those around you, where the strength you find in the Lord can encourage someone in need of support. Looking towards someone in your life for the sole origin of your happiness is only temporary and hoping that your future will change while you are holding on to this happiness is, in my opinion, not what the Lord's desire for our spirits is. I have found that the joy of the Lord is my strength; nothing compares to the promises of the power of the Holy Spirit that is my constant companion, giving me rest for my soul, where my heart can stay rooted in Him, continuing to grow towards maturity and victory.

Today I pray over my life:

John 15:10–11

"When you obey my commandments, you remain in love,

just as I obey my Father's commandments and remain in His love. I have told you these things so that you will be filled with my joy. Yes, your joy will overflow."

Let me praise Your Name as I find myself in a place where You remind me that I can rest in the knowledge that my strength is complete, through You. Thank You that I can dwell in my destiny of the revelation of Your love and joy.

A determined heart

Strength calls for a determined heart and spirit, but when life throws you into a storm, you need more than what is within yourself to claim victory. When you are close to crashing, there is support that no one else can provide, and that is found in our Warrior of Peace. Just surrender it all to Him, and darkness will fall; sickness cannot steal your joy. Raise your eyes and voice to the heavens, and do not be swayed with what is seen with your natural eyes! So, I believe that His way of reminding us of our salvation and identity is that the beautiful display of His love has redeemed us, and I can live a fully Kingdom-orientated life. I will cherish the "small" things in life that remind me of His majesty, and I can relish the amazing experiences in life, and this I will do each day, no matter what season I am in.

Resting and walking in the knowledge that I am saved is a great comfort to the peace I find in Him. My victory song can be heard above all other praises I have sung before.

I pray that my heart will play a new song, finding my everlasting freedom where I know I can find my place in Your Kingdom.

My prayer today is that I will take hold of Your hand and that I am constantly in a place of wonder and turn this around as my prayer and worship in spirit and truth. You are the light of my life; let me run into Your arms and experience Your love, mercy, and grace in a new and fulfilled way. My salvation through repentance will be my constant anchor to Your word. I can be set apart from my previous life, the unsatisfying life before becoming a new creation in Him.

I also pray the following scriptures that speak to my heart today:

Deuteronomy 30:1–3

"When all these things happen to you; the blessings and curses I have set before you and you come to your senses, while you are in the wilderness all the nations where the Lord God has driven you; and you and your children return to the Lord Your God and obey Him with all your heart and all your soul by doing everything I am giving you today; then He will restore your fortunes, have compassion on You and gather you again from all the people where the Lord God has scattered you."

My prayer is that I will take each moment I journey through life and my Christian walk as a blessing and honour to be called a child of our Abba Father. The more I know Him, I become secure, alive, whole. There is no fear when I place all my trust in Him, because He reigns forever. Do not forget that we serve a multifaceted God and knowing His character on an individual level can make our souls and spirit soar. Thank You that I have the revelation that love has a name, and His name is Jesus.

Your holiness

Today I find myself remembering the following scripture:

Psalm 91:4

"I will say of the LORD, 'He is my refuge and my fortress, my God, in whom I trust.' Surely, he will save you from the fowler's snare and from the deadly pestilence. He will cover you with his feathers, and under his wings you will find refuge; his faithfulness will be your shield and rampart."

I can still remember the moment when I surrendered to Your plan to call me under the covering of Your wings. I am so grateful that I am in a time of my life of knowing that You are aware of my heart's desire, and Your plan is to fulfil my desires in my immediate future, and this is because I am a daughter of the Highest. There is great comfort in the fact that Your plans are there to prosper me and raise me up towards Your loving arms. Let my prayers always be from a place of awe and admiration of Your holiness.

My prayer today is the following scripture:

Psalm 139: 13–15

"You made all the delicate, inner parts of my body and knit me together in my mother's womb. Thank you for making me so wonderfully complex. Your workmanship is marvellous — how well I know it. You watched me as I was formed in utter seclusion, as I was woven together in the dark of the womb.

Thank You that I have the knowledge that You, Lord, claim me as your masterpiece, thank You that I have been placed in Your caring hands. You are the God that gives, and takes away, You bless me with abundance in a world of storms, but You also take away these obstacles so that I can live without any boundaries. Thank You that the wonderful forgiveness You promise me is mine through my faith in Christ. This revelation is mine to believe, mine to treasure, mine to share. This divine message should be a constant praise on my lips, let me radiate Your love into those lives around me."

Standing strong on His promises

I can live in the promise that You expressed Your love by giving Your best, Your only Son. Sacrificing Jesus for our sins, God provided the way to reconciliation and eternal life with Him. This is an unconditional and unparalleled grace as a gift for all.

I have learnt the hard way that there are no half measures with our Abba Father; it is either that you are on fire for His Kingdom, or you are consumed with other priorities. The enemy can so easily steer us away from the word and whisper lies into Your intention for us to live in the truth of Your grace. Thankfully, Your consuming fire has guided me back to walking with the You, constantly. The Lord has been so faithful in His everlasting covenant over my loved ones that I have no choice but to live without fear, praising Him, because my faith can be rooted in His solid foundation of mercy.

I am reminded by the Holy Spirit to share the following scripture to lead me into a time of prayer: John 15:16

"You did not choose me, I choose you. I appointed you to go and produce lasting fruit, so that the Father will give you whatever you ask for, using my name."

My prayer today is that your reliance and strong faith in Him will be bigger than your fear and will guide you through this important walk of victory that we can easily obtain. Thank you that we can return our love to You and grow in our ability to love ourselves and others. The extent to which we love ourselves shapes how fully we can love others. I want to remain in a place of gratefulness that no matter how big our prayer requests are, You hear and will bring into fulfilment in Your perfect timing.

WISDOM

Filled with His wisdom

A relationship requires a lot of dedication and flexibility in beliefs, but the reward in a fulfilling relationship cannot compare to anything else. The most important relationship for me is obviously with the Lord, and the wonderful difference to our earthly ones is that the joy we find in His arms calms any storm or mountain standing in our way to grow spiritually. Trust is not easily earned, but when you finally let someone into your life and heart, there is an unspoken knowledge that you can trust them with anything. The same applies to the life we can have in our Father's arms. A foundation of trust is important in our walk with the Lord, deepening faith into a new dimension. So, stand on the strong foundation and praise His name and majesty with every breath!

Can the Lord's love disappear when we do not draw closer to Him? No, because I can live in the assurance that I can find rest for my weary soul. I have solid promises from seasons of joy, that it is a fact that He continues to love me no matter what my belief at that moment is. Let grace carry you through any situation without breaking the link to heaven's connection, bringing forth His wisdom to guide you through any season.

I pray the following scripture to resonate in my soul today:
Psalm 34
[1] I will always extol the LORD;
his praise will always be on my lips.
[2] I will glory in the LORD;
let the afflicted hear and rejoice.
[3] Glorify the LORD with me;
let us exalt his name together.
[4] I sought the LORD, and he answered me;
he delivered me from all my fears.
[5] Those who look to him are radiant;
their faces are never covered with shame.

My prayer today is that I will see His power of divine intervention in continuing to draw me closer to Him. Thank You that I can stand in awe on my righteousness and take my desire to draw nearer to His throne without condemnation. Thank You that I can walk into every situation with a radiant confidence that He guides my every step.

Staying focused on the powerful words of My Counsellor
I often feel that focusing on the challenges and obstacles in my normal day can be overwhelming. The absence of self helps to open your heart and soul to Him and ensures you are covered by His grace. You can rely on the fact that our Prince of Peace ensures that any fears will not be able to steal your joy.

The devil rejoices in the failures that we often place upon ourselves, which is a normal human trait. With repentance, we can rely on the Holy Spirit's desire to follow His prompting to enter the throne room and be guaranteed that He welcomes me without any judgement. Being real with God and laying every emotion at His feet is my refuge and answer to whatever my road looks like, always acknowledging the importance of the Holy Spirit.

Nothing happens within His hands without a reason, so I am content with the road I am on.

My prayer is based on the following scripture:

"I need Your help to silence the noise in my life. Show me which paths I must take to refocus my heart, mind, and will on You alone."

I pray today that I can live in a place of worship, because the battles I face are Yours to win, seeking Your help, where You answer without fail. Bringing You into the fight with me makes fear start to fall away. I can rely on the fact that You silence the noise in my life, making sure that I have sure footing on the foundation of faith that is my refuge. I stand in awe that You are more than willing and able to fight the hard battles with me. As I invite You into the process, dread and fear will diminish, and healing and renewal can begin.

Resting in His guided wisdom

My last entry focused on reminding me to always continue to be led by the Holy Spirit. What a great comfort it is to know that I am never alone; the gentle whisper of the heart of our Lord and Prince of Peace always soothes any darkness that tries to overpower me.

What is the way towards discerning the wonderful promises of what He has brought to our hearts? In my opinion, it is to rest in the knowledge that the Holy Spirit will define the prayers and actions for the way forward, which is easy to achieve when we apply His wisdom before we act upon a certain journey.

There are so many promises and so much guidance to build our lives on His solid foundation, that any time of spiritual attack will not be able to shake our Kingdom-planted lives. This is evident in the scripture below:

Psalm 16: 1–8

"Keep me safe, my God, for in you I take refuge.

I say to the Lord, 'You are my Lord, apart from you I have no good thing.'

I say of the holy people who are in the land, 'They are the noble ones in whom is all my delight.'

Those of you run after other gods will suffer more and more, I will not pour out libations of blood to such gods or take up their names on my lips.

Lord, you alone are my portion and my cup: you make my lot secure.

The boundary lines have fallen for me in pleasant places: surely, I have a delightful inheritance.

I will praise the Lord, who counsels me; even at night my heart instructs me.

I keep my eyes always on the Lord, with Him at my right hand, I will not be shaken."

Today I pray the following scripture over myself, and trust that you will find comfort in His word too:

Hebrews 11:3

"By faith we understand that the universe was formed at God's command, so that what is seen was not made out of what was visible."

I am thankful that I am in a place of peace because of the revelation that I will find rest for my heart and soul, being found without fail, when I look towards heaven and acknowledge Your solid standing on the rock that is higher than me. There is no name above His name and taking this to heart is an action I regularly walk by. Let your heart not grow weary; cling to our Saviour throughout your darkest day, hanging onto the Word that will guide you towards Your righteousness.

Planted where I can grow towards maturity
Today the scripture on my heart is:

Amos 9:15

"I will plant them on their land, and they will never again be uprooted from the land I have given them."

Being rooted in His promises — how wonderful is this revelation, especially in times when I feel forsaken. His guidance to build our lives on His solid foundation is a constant reminder of the sure place I have in a faith-filled life. The absence of self helps to open your heart and soul to Him and being covered by His grace, without any fears being able to steal your joy.

I will not be ashamed to declare that He is my Redeemer, and I will lean on His everlasting love and mercy that has and will stand the test of time through generations. I belong to the one and only Prince of Peace and can have solid promises from seasons of joy, that it is a fact that He continues to love me no matter what my place of spirit at that moment is. I can stand in awe on His righteousness and take my desire to draw nearer to His throne without condemnation.

My prayer today is that the following scripture will resound with your spirit:

Philippians 4:8

"And now, dear brothers and sisters, one final thing. Fix your thoughts on what is true, honorable, and right, pure, and lovely, and admirable. Think about things that are excellent and worthy of praise."

Let me continue to place my fears aside and turn my face towards the daily journey You guide me into, and there I can lift my head, walking in complete understanding that my body, soul, and spirit will be immersed in Your mercy alone. I am in a place of thankfulness because You think of me with precious thoughts.

Discernment of God

Have you ever been in a place where you experience that the devil rejoices in the failures that we often place upon ourselves, which is a normal human trait? I believe that with repentance, we can ensure that His desire for us to grow in our faith and commitment is achieved, without any judgement. That is a profound assurance that the sacred covenant we can enter into can be a refuge to take hold of.

Being real with God and laying every emotion at His feet is my refuge after spending time in His presence. Nothing happens within our lives without a reason, so I am content with the road I am on. I will continue to draw near to Him in every situation and walk in the knowledge that the establishment of His perfect plans for me will come into fulfilment. I am in a place whereby my complete faith, trust, and a sense of peace is placed before any journey where I might be in a state of uncertainty.

My prayer is that the following scripture will ensure that you are reassured of His answer to your prayers:

Psalm 7:6

"I am praying to You because I know You will answer, O God. Bend down and listen as I pray."

33

My prayer today is that I will know without a doubt that I can walk on water, and that I will see Your power of divine intervention in Your desire to continue to grow my faith from strength to strength. I will live in Your truth and let Your power shine through to guide me to spiritual maturity. Thank You that the obstacles that make me seem weak are my new strong. Thank You that my favor I find in You is like a shield, that my feet are planted beside streams of living water, seeing that You have moved my mountains. Lord, take my hand and let my spiritual eyes look towards Your promise of eternal life. Let Your power resides in my spirit; let me find a place in Your Kingdom.

Abundant life

Today, the scripture on my heart is:

Psalm 11:7

"For the righteous Lord loves justice. The virtuous will see His face."

Today, my heart is set upon this, that He has promised me an abundant life, taking in the majestic covering of the Holy Spirit. I can seek His face and be content in the fact that He, in return, sees me with His eyes, and no judgement is spoken over me. I can rest upon the wonderful realization that no weapon formed against me will prosper, because Your promises are everlasting. When I rely on Your wisdom, I can find rest for my weary soul.

My prayer today is that the following scripture will take you from strength to strength:

Romans 8:34

"Who then will condemn us? No one — for Christ Jesus died for us and was raised to life for us, and He is sitting in the place of honor at God's right hand, pleading for us."

I will declare that your justice is a mighty flood filling my spirit with a surplus of grace. I can stand on your promises that an endless river of righteous living can be a priority in my life. Be the center of my life, and let me be content in the place that I am in at the moment. I will walk beside you; Your Holy spirit is welcome and makes me strong. I will never forget how refreshing Your truth is, and I pray that this will guide me into a renewed awareness of wonder and fulfilment. Jesus listens to our request and pleads for us before our Abba Father. My strength will be the stronghold that links me to a spirit of thankfulness.

JOY

<u>Fountain of living water</u>

I am in a place of worship and want to share the following scripture:

James 1:17

"Whatever is good and perfect is a gift coming down to us from God our Father, who created all lights in heaven. He never changes or casts a shifting shadow."

What a wonderful revelation is today, that all the gifts linked to the fruits of the spirit are a gift from our Abba Father, ensuring that the cleansing that is almost always linked with water lifts my spirit. From creation to accepting Christ, through every storm and victory, we are surrounded by the living fountain of the Holy Spirit. All hurts and previous notions of what a fulfilled life must look like, wash away the moment you accept Him as your King and Prince of Peace, bringing joy to all areas of your life.

Sometimes, we tend to have high expectations from our walk with the Lord. But the minute the Lord's voice breaks through everything else clouding my mind, the "wake-up call" speaks directly to the specific season I am facing. I have experienced that in His eyes, it is necessary to cry out deeply to our Savior, Liberator and Prince of Peace, because He is there already. He always answers clearly, and with love, grace, and mercy!

So, to remind myself of my declaration to openly declare His faithfulness, shining my joy like a bright beacon, I want to focus on sharing all the heavenly riches available through grace. I want to be authentic, constantly molded by Him, and His Spirit in me should affect the radiant assurance that my thoughts and desires are known to Him. I will choose life over death; I will walk in the light of redemption and feel a sense of His unrestricted love, qualifying me as a daughter with a destiny of victory. Being mature in faith, with Christ, comes over time, and once you accept this, the Lord will continue to urge you to extend His Kingdom.

My prayer today is that I will continue to be faithful in breaking every chain in my health and in my family, and I will do so through every season, with the knowledge that I am healed, loved, cherished, and created in His image.

Everlasting covenant of joy

I have found a sense of joy in the following scripture that I want to share today:

Galatians 1:12

"I received my message from no human source, and no one taught me. Instead, I received it by direct revelation from Jesus Christ."

There is something inside me that I cannot control, making my heart sing and rejoice, for His joy in my heart is everlasting.

I was recently reminded of various scriptures around the joy of the Lord and the importance He places on our attitude and outlook over each situation. So, I am constantly trying to follow this and in doing so no mountain is too big, insurmountable, or impossible to face.

So, be encouraged with the scripture below, and

remember that His promises endure forever:

"The heavens declare the glory of God; the skies proclaim the work of his hands.

Day after day they pour forth speech; night after night they reveal knowledge.

They have no speech; they use no words; no sound is heard from them.

Yet their voices go out into all the earth, their words to the ends of the world. In the heavens God has pitched a tent for the sun.

It is like a bridegroom coming out of his chamber, like a champion rejoicing to run his course.

It rises at one end of the heavens and makes its circuit to the other; nothing is depraved of its warmth.

The law of the Lord is perfect, refreshing the soul. The statutes of the Lord are trustworthy, making wise the simple.

The precepts of the Lord are right, giving joy to the heart. The commands of the Lord are radiant, giving light to the eyes.

The fear of the Lord is pure, enduring forever. The decrees of the Lord are firm, and all of them are righteous.

They are more precious than gold, than much pure gold; they are sweeter than honey, than honey from the honeycomb.

By them your servant is warned; in keeping them there is great reward.

But who can discern their own errors? Forgive my hidden faults.

Keep your servant also from wilful sins; may they not rule over me. Then I will be blameless, innocent of great transgression."

I pray that these words of my mouth and this meditation of my heart are pleasing in your sight, Lord, my Rock and

Redeemer. I am in a place of gratitude, because Your majestic covenant has been spoken over me that will extend throughout the desert lands.

Fullness of finding joyous peace in God
The fullness I can find in my faith is linked to my intention to ensure that His calling to be either "hot" in our faith or no faith at all, which is a vital part of my soul.

We are all different in our beliefs, morals, and choices we make, but still in His eyes we are all unique, loved with an unconditional love, and seated in the Heavenly realms, without any part or action by our own doing! So, what I believe as His way of reminding us of our salvation, identity, and Kingdom orientation, is the beautiful display of the "small" things in life that turn into amazing experiences. Take each moment as you journey through life and your Christian walk as a blessing and honour to be called a child of our Abba Father.

I pray the following scripture to envelop my fears and ensure that I acknowledge the fullness of God:

Galatians 2:20

"My old self has been crucified with Christ. It is no longer I who live, but Christ lives in me. So, I live in this earthly body by trusting in the Son of God, who loved me and gave himself for me."

Thank you, Lord, that You live in me and complete me to live in the fullness of You that comes from placing my trust in You. My faith is extended when I walk in the knowledge that I am seated in the Heavenly realms.

Proclaiming praise in the foundation of joy
In my view, all of us, from creation to accepting Christ,

through every storm and victory, are surrounded by the living fountain of the Holy Spirit. All hurts and previous notions of what a fulfilled life must look like, wash away the moment you accept Him as your King and Prince of Peace. Today, I am thankful and blessed to know that Our Lord and Saviour has given us the opportunity to fall on our knees and proclaim His glory.

He has turned my life around, placing blessings before me, and there is no other joy that could compare to my life before I proclaimed His divine power. In return, it ensures that I am a new creation.

I pray the following scripture to refresh your faith in Him: Psalm 119:98–99

"Your commands make me wiser than my enemies, for they are my constant guide. Yes, I have more insight than my teachers, for I am always thinking of Your laws."

My daily prayer is that this will be evident in my walk as a Christian, and I also pray that I will continue to relish in His glory. He made a way so that my path and destiny is a known fact and revelation, and today I cherish the fact that I am a delight of the only one in the universe that matters.

Let me continue to praise His name wherever I am found by the Holy Spirit. So, stand on the strong foundation and praise His name and majesty with every breath! And let grace carry you through any situation, without breaking the link to heaven's connection. I pray that you will shout His name as a victorious acknowledgement of His presence in every detail of your day. Dance with joy and let your prayers be a delightful fragrance that the Lord is yearning for.

<u>My heart belongs to You alone</u>

I pray the following scripture over my journey with my Savior and Prince of Peace:

Psalm 19:14

"I will never fail to express the victory I have found in your loving embrace. You are my rock and redeemer."

My heart belongs to You only; my devotion is Yours alone. Seeing Your hand in my journey brings a life-changing understanding to see myself as You do, making all things new. Jesus, I long for Your love; all I want is to be satisfied by Your presence, as only You can. Let my awareness of You be a constant revelation of the path You have placed before me. Your desire for me is not to be weary and seek rest in this world, but You allow Your grace and mercy to ensure that all I need to be a victorious daughter of the Highest is You. You pour out the oil of joy; Your face is turned towards me, filling me with a peaceful heart.

My prayer today is the following scripture:

Psalm 8:1

"Lord, our Lord, how magnificent is Your name throughout the earth! You have covered the heavens with Your majesty."

My prayer today is that I can have a heartful feeling of gratefulness that You are my Prince of Peace, my firm foundation, and the rock on which I can stand in righteousness. I will continue to speak truth into every season that You have led me into. Let my words never contradict the promises You have laid down before me. Let me always hold onto the truth that I am rooted in my salvation that I can only find in You. Thank You that You do not disqualify me because I am in the early days of my faith. You teach me, purpose me, use me from the start of salvation. Your word makes the difference, illuminating who Jesus is and God's incredible plans for me. Nothing else brings Your radiance and turns up my light of righteousness.

Let His tangible joy fulfil you
Nothing in this world is ever really considered as forever, unless you are living with the certainty of Him who lives in You and died for you! Are you blessed and in a place where this wonderful fact is such an important part of your life that anyone that asks you, are you a child of God, you can answer immediately, yes?

If you can answer yes without a doubt, is that not a reason enough to shout it from the streets, mountains, wherever your path takes you, that you remain to yearn to be closer to Him, letting hope arise? I will let my joy, freedom, and identity in Him be so tangible that I am able to live in a place of praise, worshipping His name and the majestic wonders He has placed before me.

I pray the following scripture that overflows the trusting spirit in my heart:
Hebrews 6:19
"This hope is a strong and trustworthy anchor for our souls. It leads us through the curtain into God's inner sanctuary."

My hope lies in the expectation that I will continue to take my greatest comfort that the chance to anchor my soul to the revelation that I can enter His inner sanctuary cannot be cut short with the inevitable way life gets in the way of truly seeking His kingdom first.

PERFECT TIMING

<u>Not forsaken</u>

The scripture on my heart today is:

Psalm 115:1

"Not to us, O Lord, not to us, but to Your name goes all the glory for Your unfailing love and faithfulness."

The things I am grateful for:

1. My close relationship with You.
2. The ability to kneel before You.
3. Being pulled away from the shadows in life.
4. That my heart can hold onto You, deepening my voice of worship.

What I want to ask of God:

    a. Give me more patience when I run away from the power of prayer.
    b. Never let go of me.
    c. I want to intervene on behalf of my loved ones, to draw closer to You.

I will commit to the gentleness of God to answer the desires of my heart. He always answers clearly and with the covenant of salvation as the ultimate prize. I will rely on my steadfast perseverance to increase my faith on a continuous basis. Lord, what a difference it is to dwell in Your presence, living in truth with the revelation that You are my everything.

Let Your presence rain on me, refreshing my soul, being aligned with Your Word.

I am sure that You celebrate every moment with me, even those I consider as failures or problems, as You use them to teach me a way out of darkness. Those in Your eyes are what builds my faith, bringing me closer to You. You shower me with all the love that I need and then some more. You are my God of hope, love, joy, peace, understanding, warrior of all ages, and without You in my heart, spirit and life, no other entity can compare to the power of my salvation.

My prayer today is that the scripture that brings about a sense of peace will also fill your heart with an understanding of His grace:

Psalm 130:5

"I am counting on the Lord; yes, I am counting on Him. I have put my hope in His word."

I can kneel before You. My almighty God is my fortress, and You never remain silent or distant from me. The strong foundation that I am rooted in as Your beloved daughter, calms my spirit and renews my strength. Let my song to heaven arise with my victorious revelation of being held in Your embrace of love, grace and mercy.

His voice

Today, the scripture on my heart is:

Isaiah 30:15

"In repentance and rest is your salvation, in quietness and trust is your strength."

I often ponder on how I can remain in a place of quietness to grasp the message that God wants me to be an individual, strengthened by my faithfulness, trusting Him completely. I am grateful that His love always speaks to my heart in every beautiful experience and encounter where He meets me. He knows our divine destiny, past, present, and future. He knows in what stage or season we are in. There is no other fact that remains but to give my most in serving and making a change in His Kingdom!

My prayer is that the following scripture will remind you of His grace:

Micah 7:7

"As for me, I look to the Lord for help. I wait confidently for God to save me, and my God will certainly hear me."

My prayer today is that I will remain close to His heart that reminds me that His love will ensure that I can stand strong on the promises I have prayed for daily, and those that He knows before we do, and my belief is that this is also true towards every believer. His loving whispers ensure that we can be assured that our day of tomorrow is rooted and is held in His hand with unfailing grace. Persevere in walking into the new day with the certainty that you can listen to His whispers and know that you can reach out in every circumstance.

Waiting on the Lord to fulfil His promises
The revelation that a season of trusting for His perfect timing will bring about is that the words in my soul will resonate with the truths to fulfil each of the many promises that are true to His word. You have never disappointed me, because I place my trust in You. My priorities are to set Jesus at the centre of all that I hope for, and this is a sure recipe for bringing glory to His name. Let this be a guiding light into the future that awaits me. My strength is my anchor for ensuring that every

moment has been enforced by Your powerful hand, and I will remain in this place of identity.

You are consistent in Your graceful love that is still such a wonder, that brings me to my knees and is expressed through my praises. When I acknowledge that Your divine power and destiny is for me, and behind me, and upholds me, there will be no mountain too high for me to defeat any strongholds over me.

Your word promises me that I will see the light for the one that holds on, and that is a wonderful revelation that refreshes me and creates a sense of amazement in my soul. You are the King of creation, placing each one of us at the feet of Jesus. You loved us unconditionally and sacrificed everything so that I can be victorious in the life that was planned and spoken over me since the beginning of creation.

I was reminded of the following uplifting scripture:

Psalm 18:6

"I called to the Lord in my distress and cried out to the Lord for help. From His temple He heard my voice and my cry to Him reached His ears."

I also pray that the confidence I find in the boldness of my faith will be the anthem to my song of praise, shouting this aloud. I want to wait to become more rooted in the strength that comes from You alone. I am in a place of worship because You have never let go of me, through the calm and through the storm. I will be quiet to sense the direction Your Holy Spirit is leading and guiding me to. Let me live in the here and now; let Your love wash over me, cleansing me so that my sins are forgiven. Let me not be worried about the day of tomorrow but find rest for my soul in Your promise of healing and peace.

Your mercy knows no boundaries; I speak revival over my walk with You.

Thank you, Lord, that I can conquer everything through You, and that you see every tear that I shed considering the many difficulties I endure but am still afraid of giving over to You. Let me know the difference between the unrestricted mercy You want me to rely on and not be overshadowed by the struggles of this world. I know that You will give me the power of inner strength so that my entire life will be built on the love that flows from You.

Choices

The scripture placed before me today is:

1 Peter 5:8–11

"Be self-controlled and alert. Your enemy, the devil, prowls around like a roaring lion looking for someone to devour. Resist him, standing firm in your faith."

With this in mind, I want to continue to be authentic, constantly shaped by You, creating a sense of awareness to fight against any plans the devil has to steal me away from my victory and destiny. The Holy Spirit in me must affect what I think, feel, and the choices that I make. Being mature in faith, with Christ, comes over time, and once I realised this, the Lord has continued to urge me to extend His Kingdom and place this as a priority in order for me to stand in a place of worship before Him.

You still amaze me. Your grace is a joyous wonder, and Your strength and mercy will guide me through any valley in my path.

There is a great feeling of peace when I look back at Your love towards me, knowing with full confidence that Your purpose for me has always been to be loved beyond my understanding, making the right choices that will fill me with a sense of peace, knowing that I am not forsaken. Hope, peace, and love are just a few emotions that carry me through any situations that I may and have faced.

Today, I pray the following scripture to remain my constant anchor to my salvation:

Psalm 27:9

"Do not turn Your back on me. Do not reject Your servant in anger. You have always been my helper. Don't leave me now; don't abandon me, O God of my salvation."

Today, I pray that I will rely on Your strength to fight against the devil. I want to heed to the gentle whisper of Your voice to guide me towards my destiny. Thank you that I can live in a place of victory, and that Your ways are loving and faithful towards me, because I keep the demands of our covenant. I can hide myself in Your grace and experience Your presence wherever I am. Thank You that I can hold onto the truth of my existence and rejoice in it. I will become a "possibility thinker", never underestimating the power of Your hand in my walk, drawing me closer to You.

Ever-present God

The scripture on my heart today is:

Hebrews 6:19

"This hope is strong and a trustworthy anchor for our souls. It leads us through the curtain into God's inner sanctuary."

I will have faith in Your anchor that You have freely given me. Let me draw closer to my deeply rooted foundation to Your Kingdom in order for me to walk into Your amazing sanctuary. Your promise of my hope in You is better than anything that this world can offer me. I will never stop believing that I am rooted in my ever-present God's loving embrace. The value of persistent prayer is not that He hears us but that we will finally hear Him.

I pray the following scripture over my life and the path that my loved ones are on:

Psalm 28:2

"Listen to my plea for mercy, as I lift my hands toward your holy sanctuary."

I also feel led by the spirit that I should be in a place of worship, relying on the fact that I will never stop seeing His hand in the majestic creation of our wonderful world. To all creation I will sing; I will be a faithful servant in the midst of any season I find myself in.

Thank You that I can walk into the curtain of redemption into Your inner sanctuary.

I keep on falling in love with You; You alone are my God. I pray that You will never let me go and that I will continue to trust that Your desire for my right standing will be a sure revelation.

<u>Following with a heart full of obedience</u>

He has given us the opportunity to fall on our knees and proclaim His glory, being in an intimate relationship, because we can proclaim the importance of His presence. There is no other peace than the one that comes from the knowledge that all our iniquities are crushed by His blood. When you need perspective and guidance, the perfect place to be at is at Jesus's feet, praying that your faith will pull you through whatever your request is. He showers us with all the love that we need and then some more, He is our God of Hope, Love, Joy, Peace, Understanding, Warrior of all ages.

The scripture I find comfort in is found in:

Jeremiah 33:6

"Behold, I will bring them health and healing; I will heal them and reveal to them the abundance of peace and truth."

I pray today that you will turn towards Him with expectation, trusting that He knows your needs and will bring abundant healing to your soul. I pray that you will position all your burdens at His feet and look towards your future, finding peace in a place of serenity. I trust that you will be obedient to the leading of the Holy Spirit and place His Kingdom before anything else. Our God is a jealous God and longs for us to be an instrument of glory.

Opening your spiritual eyes

My experience during these past few years is that I can have the boldness to enter His throne room, because I do not have to conform to the way of this world. I am constantly reminded that when I see His glory with my spiritual eyes, I can feel my heart being softened with His mercy. I can have faith that He will deal with all my needs for that specific situation on my heart.

We do not have to feel that our difficulties are impossible to conquer. I keep His promises close to my heart, and I stand in amazement in His presence, feeling content in the position of righteousness He has placed before me, without any conditions I need to fulfill on my part.

The scripture that resonates with my spirit is:

Psalm 36:9

"For You are the fountain of life, the light by which we see."

I also pray, Lord, that I will continue to be a faithful follower of Your word, and give me the assurance of living in your light, being strong through every situation. I will be receptive to Your gentle guidance to open our spiritual eyes to have the full assurance of His mercy. Bless my life with Your everlasting love, peace, and grace. Thank You that You are the fountain of life, keeping Your promise that a refreshing spirit is easily available. Let me remain in a place of worship and live in the truth of my salvation.

BEAUTY

His majestic creation
How wonderful He has made everything around us; I can only stand in amazement seeing all the beauty that surrounds me. I always stand in reverence, looking at all the amazing ways the Lord shows us His power and His desire for us to be surrounded by all this beauty. He has created us to marvel in the right standing we can have when we call upon His name as our rock of redemption.

I continue to find my refuge in immersing myself in the small things in nature, and the knowledge that He has great experiences to share with me. I do not know what the day of tomorrow will bring, but I know that He will be right beside me. I can proclaim today that the songs of the harmony of nature's sounds will remind me of who my Creator is. It has taken me a long time to come to this revelation, and in the background the Lord has been waiting patiently for this to resonate in my spirit. I am incredibly awed at how He never remains silent, and I will keep on praising His name in every situation I am in.

And of course, it is not always as easy as we desire, but when we acknowledge that His divine power and destiny is for us and behind us, there is no mountain or valley too high to overcome. I have made another, yet again, commitment to walk in truth, accepting and acknowledging His love and direction into my destiny. I believe to achieve the beauty of His covenant with me is to make a conscious decision every day to:

- Stop living in neutral mode.
- Stop living in apology of my past mistakes.
- Walk my road without the burdens of misconceptions of what makes me perfect.

Even in promising myself all the above-mentioned critical steps, I still face a constant struggle to remain focused on my commitment to accept my Lord as my Redeemer. Sadly, sometimes this has been overshadowed by the demands of my day-to-day walk with the Lord. Surely, obedience to His prompting must take centre stage. His face still shines towards me.

I pray the following scripture over my day and my current journey:

Isaiah 61:3a

"To all who mourn in Israel, he will give a crown of beauty from ashes, a joyous blessing instead of mourning, festive praise instead of despair."

I am in a place of wonder with the revelation that we have the wrong belief that goodness and beauty are in the eye of the beholder, but in our wonderful world of our Creator, it is in His eyes that our goodness and beauty is evident. It is a tangible, wonderful blessing that will draw me closer to His loving embrace. He reveals himself in the road of deliverance, ensuring that my spirit can be transformed from ashes to beauty.

GRACE

Place of shelter

Today, the scripture on my heart is:

Psalm 95:1–3

"Come, let us sing to the Lord! Let us shout joyfully to the Rock of our salvation. Let us come to Him with thanksgiving. Let us sing psalms of praise to Him. For the Lord is a great God. A great King above all gods."

His grace is sufficient; I can declare that I can focus on a place of shelter, which is freely given to us, from the minute that we are born into this world. The covering of His grace has been planned to ensure that the availability of His mercy is open to those that have a desperate need for this. More than anything, we can let creation testify His majesty, finding rest in the wonder of it. How amazing is the knowledge that the Lord takes pleasure in giving us so many blessings and glimpses into His creation!

I am always brought to a sense of wonder that life is never predictable, and when I am entangled in struggles to cope with everyday life, His grace and mercy, marrying all the gifts He showers us with the right attitude, makes a world of difference!

I stumbled across an entry on my Facebook profile recently, and our Abba Father just brought across my path again, as always, just what I needed to hear and believe. It is as follows:

"Waves are inspiring, not because they rise and fall but because each time they fall, they never fail to rise again." — Ralph Waldo Emerson.

What a wonderful gift from above, His grace and mercies never fail me. We all need to hear and believe in His word to carry us through the deep waters, or for us to rejoice in the graceful abundance we find ourselves in. How wonderful it is to face life,with the knowledge that my salvation is guaranteed, that my Redeemer has paid the ultimate price to ensure eternal life has been granted to me. I know that He will reclaim us and place us before our Heavenly Father to rejoice on the day of His return. Heaven will accept us with open arms, and I am sure that it will be a moment of joy where I can fall on my knees and give Him all the glory. No other person can love me as much as He does, my Saviour and King.

Remember to always continue to be led by the Holy Spirit, and at the same time, read what He has brought to your heart, through His wisdom, before you act upon a certain journey.

I pray the following scripture to take root with a renewed sense of awareness of the power of His grace:

Psalm 63:7

"Because You are my help, I sing in the shadow of Your wings."

My prayer is that you will run towards Him, even if you feel that everyday life runs away from you. Step into the role in His kingdom that was intended all along. He can renew your strength in those areas that you think are impossible. Trust in Him, surrounded and encircled by His grace. As we worship our Saviour and King, He goes before us and ensures that whatever our heart is being consumed with will be taken care of. He is omnipresent, His grace everlasting, and His only request is that we follow Him with all our heart, spirit, and mind.

Remain in a place of trust that your belief is secure in the fact that the extent of His love is something that cannot be explained; everything else in this world does not measure up to the feeling of peace that we can call upon, in whichever place you are in. Thank You, Lord, that we can realise the impact of Your promise to have the boldness to declare that any challenge disappears in the face of Your saving grace.

Christ lives in me

The following scripture is on my heart today:

Galatians 2:20

"I have been crucified with Christ and no longer live, but Christ lives in me."

I thank You today with the revelation that I became less, and You became more, because Christ lives in me, and I can declare without a doubt that I am a daughter in Your heavenly Kingdom.

I want to live according to Your heart, hiding my fears in Your light, while I wait upon Your declaration of love and grace. Making my ears open to fully understand the way You want to reveal Your love into every situation is my main objective in my current season. I want to just take a moment and look above, around me, and lastly within me. I can hear the sound as angels gather around, welcoming me home.

My soul clings to You because of my salvation. Let my praise be a gentle whisper relaying the truth that I find in Your word, persevering in faith, being sensitive to the prompting to experience the promises You have in store for me. I perceive them, because my resting place of worship when I rely on Your word is a solid foundation, rooting me to Your peace. I am grateful when I realise that I have been given the power to come out of any darkness in my life triumphantly. There is healing under the covering of Your wings of grace and mercy. You have given me a purpose with each obstacle I face, and I have seen Your hand in the way You shape me into a new creation. You do not want me to live my faith out in isolation, but You ask that I place Your Kingdom above all else, in order to touch the lives of those around me, and let the light I am living in shine through any darkness others experience. I can do this because I carry Your victory granted to all of us, unconditionally.

I declare the following scripture that I found over my day now:

John 14:26

"But when the Father sends the Advocate as my representative — that is, the Holy Spirit — He will teach you everything and will remind you of everything I have told you."

My prayer is that I will remain in a place of worship, running to You with a certainty that You are already transforming my dreams into reality. You have been fighting my battles throughout the beginning of time. What You open, no one can close, and what You close, no one can open. Thank You that there is a revelation through Your Holy Spirit that I am saved.

You place before me blessings and a glimpse into the road into victory, and this reaffirms my identity as a loved and cherished servant, which will continue to ensure I have a close relationship with You. I will be in a place of thanksgiving; I give up control, because there is no one else I want to lean on; You carry me. Because You have revealed yourself with the reminder of the grace You poured out into my life, my spirit will rejoice with songs of praise. Let me dance for joy, because You speak life into my soul, throughout all the steps of transferring pain into ever-comforting peace, creating in me a sense of being a new creation.

What a wonderful comfort it is to know that I can run towards Your grace and fall to my knees when Satan whispers that I am forsaken. I will live my life in Your beautiful light; my steps are not shadowed in darkness, for this boldness that You have freely given me will be my anthem song of praise. I declare that I will not be shaken by any obstacles.

Lord, I also pray that I will live in a place of thankfulness: because You have heard my plea, my weeping is not in vain. I declare Your mercy, grace, and peace over my day. Let Your will be done. Believing and declaring Your place in my life is a constant reminder of Your everlasting grace.

I will abide in Your word without starting another new season of growth. For the one who was and is to come will continue to be a joyful song of praise for me. I will acknowledge that You are the one I bow before, and that You reign endlessly.

TRANSFORMATION

<u>Introduction</u>

The scripture on my heart today is:

1 Peter 2:9

"But you are a chosen race, a royal priesthood, a holy nation, a people for His own possession, that you may proclaim the excellencies of Him who called you out of darkness into His marvelous light."

The story of our lives is the product of our Creator, drawing us out of darkness and requesting us to trust that He will bring a transformation to our identity. He has helped me through many trials and tribulations, and even in the light of this, it is sometimes so easy to be caught up in the things of this world. Once I placed all my trust in giving over every part of my soul and mind, the relationship I found in Him has been the most important treasure I will ever have, being a constant source of feeling loved and placed in right standing with the ultimate prize of redemption. Jesus has paid the ultimate sacrifice in order for us to live in the knowledge that no other love is greater than His, my King of glory.

I want to pray the following scripture over myself today:

Isaiah 43:19

"For I am about to something new. See, I have already begun! I will make a pathway through the wilderness. I will create rivers in the dry wasteland."

I also pray that the solid relationship, as a child of God, must be the priority in all things that my soul is consumed with. I will lay all the broken pieces at His feet and know that any situation is taken care of. This is the purpose of His love — creating a pathway through the wilderness, giving us the endurance to reach the glorious fountain of life found where our thirst takes us.

Break my heart for what breaks yours

A favourite lyric that has always remained at the centre of my belief is "Break my heart for what breaks yours" from a song called Hosanna produced by Hillsong, with the words and music by Brooke Fraser. I believe this relates to how we live life and show our desire to accept His direction in making a difference in other believer's hearts, but most importantly, those that have not experienced the salvation and redemption of the Holy Spirit. My dreams and visions are that they will experience the peace and a place of welcome that comes with His gentleness.

I believe that when we make the most important decision to worship Him and acknowledge His redeeming love and the transformation that it brings, we will be complete in Him.

I pray that the following scripture will create a sense of peace over my day:

Genesis 28:15

"I am with you and will keep you wherever you go. For I will not leave you until I have done what I promised you."

Thank You that I can live fully in the knowledge that You, Abba Father, have, and always will, restore my fortunes. You have compassion on me, because I choose the many blessings, and not curses, that You have placed before me. I will forever praise Your name, because the most important decision to worship You and acknowledge Your redeeming mercy has created a heart filled with awe and wonder. Let my positioning of redemption be a constant song of praise, lifting Your name up high. There is no other name above Your name.

I also pray that I will be in a place of celebration of who God is, what He has done, and rejoice in all He has in store for me.

Transformed through the work of the cross.
The following scripture comes into the meditation of my heart:
>"And yet, o Lord, You are our Father. We are the clay, and
>You are the potter. We all are formed by Your hand,"

He is our Lamb, truth and Jesus. These three words stand out so vividly lately, and with reason: Jesus paid the ultimate sacrifice for you and me to live in His truth, and not just saying we live, but living it out in our walk every day! His anointment shines upon my face. I am no longer running through the night, walking in the shadows, but His light shows me the road to redemption, with His unfailing grace and everlasting love being my comforter and healer. My soul clings to Him; because of my salvation, let my praise be a gentle whisper relaying the truth that I find in Your word, persevering in faith, being sensitive to the prompting to experience the promises You have in store for me. Let me acknowledge the transformation You bring to the deepest depths, and that my faith in You will continue to grow, creating a thankful spirit in me.

I pray the following scripture to ensure my new transformation remains my main focus:

Psalm 25:10

"All the ways of the Lord are loving and faithful
toward those who keep the demands of his covenant."

I also pray that when I am in a place of praising You, Lord, that You will ensure that no matter what I face, restoration will take place, constantly and without fail. I am no longer running through the night, walking in the shadows, but Your light shows me the road to redemption, Your unfailing grace and everlasting love. My soul clings to You because of my salvation. Let my praise resonate with the gentle whisper of the Holy Spirit, relaying the truth that I find in Your word, persevering in faith, being sensitive to the prompting to experience the promises You have in store for me. Let us acknowledge the transformation You bring to the deepest depths, in order for our faith in Him to continue to grow from strength to strength. I also pray that we will declare boldly the victory that is ours.

From a place of redemption

During a difficult time of my journey as a daughter of the most High, I had a very vivid dream that brought a new perspective into the heart of Jesus.

I saw myself struggling in my own strength (the little I had) through a maze of dry rosebushes, but as I turned one last corner, desperate for someone to save me, I heard the Lord whispering that well-known verse Psalm 46:10; "Be still and know that I am God." As I surrendered ALL to Him, seeing myself through His eyes, I distinctly felt certain of my identity, inheritance, and salvation.

I saw the path I have been walking from Heaven's perspective, and the maze is in a heart shape, transformed into abundant green leaves, flowers, and the most beautiful stream of water in the center of it. The revelation that came with this vision is that all my fountains are in Him! Those words have been on my lips in church during worship for so many months, although only without a heart of understanding. This dream ensured that I could live in the everlasting covenant of healing and brought me under the covering of my righteousness.

I pray the following scripture today:

Hebrews 4:15–16

"This High Priest of ours understands our weaknesses, for He faced all of the same testing we do, yet He did not sin. So, let us come boldly to the throne of our gracious God. There we will receive His mercy, and we will find grace to help us when we need it most."

Let me rely on His strength and gentle prompting to be bold enough to draw closer to Him. I find rest for my soul, because a deeper understanding of the work of the cross has been a sure foundation of my faith. Today, I can shout it out with full confidence in who I am, and to whom I belong, relishing in the knowledge of my restoration. I can have a spirit filled with gratefulness because I can find grace in the core of any storm.

Complete in Him

I believe that when we make the most important decision to worship Him and acknowledge His redeeming love and the transformation that it brings, we will be complete in Him.

Have you ever unconsciously considered why our lives take a certain direction before we really listen to our God?

In a time of listening for the prompting of the Lord's whisper of confirmation that His hand is guiding me, I had a clear understanding of the above question. The following illustration came to mind, whereby I saw a beautiful tree with a twisted trunk.

With this in mind, I guess you can say that before I accepted Christ as my saviour, my life and the person I was could be seen as a "tree" that was also twisted, but His plan to shape me into His new creation came to fruition the day I surrendered my spirit to Him. One of my favourite gospel lyrics says "You are the thirst, you are the hunger, you are the food that satisfies," from the song, You Are Everything (Everything I Need) written by Brian Doerksen so in my heart it is a continual circle of seeking and finding all my needs, desires and dreams in Him.

Again, I am reminded of the word that says, found in Ephesians 6:10"n conclusion, be strong in the Lord, draw your strength from Him and be empowered through your union with Him, and in the power of His boundless might".

I guess you could say it is an everlasting cycle with the most wonderful freedom you can ever experience, if only we consider to not let the following issues overwhelm us:

• Worry when your day and plans do not work out as you planned.

• Be ill-tempered when your loved ones do not love you the way you expect them to, but know that His love endures forever.

• Concern yourself with the attitudes and actions of the persons in your life that you least expect it from; you cannot carry or lessen their hurt, or even explain it!

• Try to be perfect. No one can say they are; this is just fooling yourself. We are perfect and righteous ONLY because of what Jesus did on the cross!

• Your focus being unbalanced; being concerned about life and not living it to the glory of God. In my belief, this would definitely mean that we produce few good fruits.

What does your tree, and fruit, look like?

I pray the following scripture to align with the place of worship I am in:

Matthew 12: 33–35

"Either make the tree good and its fruit good, or make the tree bad and its fruit bad, for a tree is known by its fruit. Brood of vipers! How can you speak good things when you are evil? For the mouth speaks from the overflow of the heart. A good man produces good things from his storeroom of good, and an evil man produces bad things from his storeroom of evil.

I tell you that on the day of judgement people will have to account for every careless word they speak. For by your words, you will be acquitted, and by your words you will be condemned".

My prayer today is to acknowledge that a resting place for my spirit will change my deeds from passive to active, finding a way to elevate Your name, bringing glory. Become the "possibility thinker". Be an instrument of GLORY!

Placing His Kingdom first

During a quiet time, a while ago, concerning the scripture below, I had a sense that once the Lord calls you towards your identity, and you truly recognize Him as your Saviour and Provider for all your needs, that placing His Kingdom first will be a focus that will strengthen your spirit.

John 1 v. 35–42

35 The next day John was there again with two of his

disciples.

36 When he saw Jesus passing by, he said, "Look, the Lamb of God!"

37 When the two disciples heard him say this, they followed Jesus.

38 Turning around, Jesus saw them following and asked, "What do you want?" They said, "Rabbi" (which means "Teacher"), "where are you staying?"

39 "Come," he replied, "and you will see." So, they went and saw where he was staying, and they spent that day with him. It was about four in the afternoon.

40 Andrew, Simon Peter's brother, was one of the two who heard what John had said and who had followed Jesus.

41 The first thing Andrew did was to find his brother Simon and tell him, "We have found the Messiah" (that is, the Christ).

42 And he brought him to Jesus. Jesus looked at him and said, "You are Simon son of John. You will be called Cephas" (which, when translated, is Peter).

In this scripture, Jesus called his disciples to come and "see", and to follow Him, they first had to hear and decide on the road going forward, and once they saw again where He was staying, they decided to follow Him. Andrew was also told of this, and once he arrived, he was renamed — by Jesus, so a new identity was implied — the revelation that I spoke about earlier concerning identity.

What I feel the Holy Spirit is guiding me into is that seeing is believing, and your spiritual eyes need to be open, and your heart and soul should be receptive to the Holy Spirit to lead you into the way forward. Your main concern and outlook on life will never remain the same, but the struggles and issues unfortunately never disappear. I also believe that the perfect life for a Christian, as the world believes, does not exist, unless you surrender all your thoughts and struggles over to Your Prince of Peace, our God of answered prayers.

But we have the assurance that a method and solution to all questions and concerns is available, and that placing your trust in Him can ensure that the close relationship with the Holy Trinity that calms every storm will bring everlasting peace.

Is the Lamb of God your truth, or are you still waiting to make that choice?

My prayer today is the following Psalm:
"You, O Lord, don't hide yourself, your heart for me never stays silent.

You, O Lord, don't only speak while I am listening, You are patient and teach lessons for our own good."

With this in mind, I can thank You, Lord, for guiding my spirit towards Your loving arms. Thank You, Lord, for never taking my past into account while You pour out Your blessings to overflowing abundance.

You have promised us a future and everlasting love, and I can live in the freedom that is beyond comparison. I will praise your name in everything I am, do, think, and speak. You call us to be humble, never forgetting that seeking the Kingdom, above all else, is a vital part of living free, and in His eyes, we can be perfect, righteous, and loved beyond measure, and that we will have a clear destiny.

Revelations on a new creation
I am in a place of contemplation, as this is a celebration of two important journeys that I have been led onto, as this is the tenth

anniversary of my first encounter with breast cancer. I have a revelation in constantly believing that the way the Lord has carried not only me, but all my loved ones, must never be taken for granted. He will give you the strength and wisdom to fight with all your heart to overcome any struggle.

One of the requirements of our journeys is that we must answer the calling He has prayed over us, creating a child-like faith, without fail. The revelation that has really sunk into my soul is that the words that the medical profession declares over your body cannot withstand the healing power that the Lord wants for you. Why should we be concerned about their diagnosis, when our doctor, Abba Father, places the promise of restoration and healing when we are in a place of needing His healing touch?

The second painful path is that this is unfortunately also the month that my mom was taken from us in September 2017, also due to breast cancer. The longing for just one more encounter where we can share our memories throughout our time spent together, of laughing and talking, is an ache that has been with me since her passing. Thankfully, I know that she is constantly with me in spirit, and I am reminded that I loved her in the living, and I cherish this revelation every day.

The scripture I would like to pray over my heart today is: 1 John 3:1a

"See how very much our Father loves us, for He calls us His children, and that is what we are."

I pray that we will remember that who you are and what you do are two different places you will find yourself in. I believe that what He has spoken over His children's lives is always a new beginning, making available everything in the Kingdom without end. There is no other name like our Saviour and King. I am thankful every day that I can call upon His Name for help and that He will come to my rescue, placing forgiveness in my path of righteousness.

Rejoicing in the moments of His loving arms

A while ago I was on my way home, when a little girl was riding on her bicycle, and her dad was driving by. She raced to catch up with him, shouting "Yay, Daddy is home." I had the feeling that this joy, as a daughter of the Most High, is probably the same that the Lord speaks over us, when we return home upon making the important decision to take hold of our salvation. Living out the truth that we have an abundant light, that others wonder about, should remain a focus to impact fellow believers.

I revel in the prompting of the Holy Spirit on the following scripture:

Psalm 119:93

"I will never forget Your commandments, for by them You give me life."

My prayer today is that I will rely on my spirit-filled prayer life as a guiding light. Place Him first in your life, believing that through Him nothing is impossible. Be open to sharing your walk as a child of God, continuing to acknowledge the solid foundation of His love and mercy. Show kindness to everyone you encounter, for it can be a turning point for someone to see His hand in giving a new meaning to their life. Remain rooted to His promise of giving us light to show us the way out of darkness.

Bending time

Today the scripture on my heart is:

John 17:21(As in the words of Jesus to His disciples)

"May they all be one, as You, Father, are in me and I am in You. May they also be one in us, so the world may believe You sent me."

I am in a place of praise because the inspiration I find in Your word today brings forth the following truths:

You can bend time and events in my current situation, as well as in my future. I see the cloud of salvation rise; whatever the cost, I will follow You with a spirit of high praise. In a place of wonder, I will find my destiny. You created and established my world by Your wisdom. Let me remain rooted in the revelation and let me be astonished by the journey You have planned, asking me to be committed to You alone.

When I make the most important decision to worship You and acknowledge Your redeeming love and the transformation that it brings, I will be complete in Him. Your only request is to make room in my day to move my heart by the guiding, gentle whisper that speaks to my fears. There are no failures that are too strong to overwhelm me and steal me away from the intention of Your redemption.

I pray the following scripture to release a song of praise today:

"I pray today that I will cherish the fact that the most beautiful sound in the world to me is the gentle whisper of Your guidance."

I pray that I will see the light of deliverance, because my heart will hold onto You. I pray that all Your children will return to Your loving arms. Let the darkness fade and guide their song of praise to have an expectation of grace and Your unconditional love. Thank you that the favor we can find in You is like a shield. Jesus, You are still enough, and this can be our confidence that we will see You move the mountains, and I believe we will see it move without end.

I also pray that You will fill us with renewed strength to walk out of darkness and revel in the comfort of Your light. Let our silence be something in the past. Let our songs of praise be a joyous moment in a new season; let us dance with a soft melody of Your love and grace. Your word says that if we put our delight in You, You will grant us our heart's desires. This is such a wonderful eye-opener; we can marinate our hearts in the power of this promise.

I lift Your name high; I will worship You without limits, and I pray that my heart full of thanksgiving will be a worthy offering.

You have compassion on me, because I choose the many blessings, and not curses, that You have placed before me. I will forever praise Your name, because the most important decision to worship You and acknowledge Your redeeming mercy and grace will lead me on a path of salvation and redemption. Thank You that I know that You accept my prayers, bringing forth answers that resonate within me. I find fullness when the Holy Spirit speaks to me, and I will behold it and realize that it is poured out in the here and now, taking every season and leading me to understand the struggles that You released me from any strongholds. I will testify to the revival I find in You.

I pray the following scripture to echo in my heart:
Psalm 30:12
"That I might sing praises to You, and not be silent. O Lord my God, I will give thanks forever."

MY IDENTITY

Taking comfort in my destiny

The scripture that I have meditated on today is:

Jeremiah 1:5

"Before I formed you in the womb, I knew you, and before you were born, I consecrated you; I have appointed you a prophet of nations."

To know that I am always welcome in His presence is a comfort like no other. That phrase "Let go and let God" is also a great truth that I lean on deeply. I relish in the fact that in You lies my identity, my Abba Father, my Prince of Peace. Let me revel in the prophecy You have spoken over me; let me have the discernment to be in a place of worship and not feel forsaken.

I have a thankful heart, for my many blessings:

- My health.
- The fellowship that will draw me closer to You!
- My provision.
- My blessed family and loved ones.

With my new season in full swing, the majesty of Your creation is still a wonder in my life. I am constantly reminded that He never hides His face and that His identity and grace for me are always present. How wonderful is the realization that all my fountains are in Him! Those words have been on my lips in church during worship for so many years, and I can now proclaim that I will continue to let them reverberate in my soul. You are my rock, my fortress and the One I adore. You are the hunger, the thirst, and the food that satisfies, bringing forth a path of promises my heart can take comfort in.

Living water springs up in my life, increasing as each day, hour, minute turns into a life of an everlasting covenant, with Your plans to prosper me and not to harm me. Today, I can shout out with full confidence in who I am and to whom I belong to. I trust that the same can be applied to the lives of others.

I pray the following scripture to resonate with my spirit today:

Ephesians 5:19

"Singing psalms and hymns and spiritual songs among yourselves, and making music to the Lord in your hearts."

My prayer today is that I am thankful that I am part of Your Kingdom. You have raised me up from darkness, so that I can live in Your truth and shine the light of my soul into existence. How can I ever thank You enough for what You have done for me? I will be still and know that You are my God; You are a God of mercy, and I take refuge in knowing that my rightful place in heaven has been prepared, lifting me up so that I can grow from weary to strong. I will continue to sing psalms and hymns to glorify Your name and for what You have done in my spiritual life. My heart will sing a new song every morning, raising me up towards the feet of Jesus.

Deepening your faith to find the place of your destiny
Do you feel that life often brings some difficulties that make you forget His promises?

In my experience, I realise that I do not have to be caught

up in my mind's ability to struggle with being in a place of abandonment. I have often found myself in a place where it sometimes is hard to comprehend that the covering of His grace of everything in my journey towards fullness is so readily available. We can find worldly fullness in our loved ones or the joys of life, but with gratitude I can cancel my belief that everything that is right is not in these material things. During these times, I feel that nothing washes away these concerns as much as believing in Your prayer, as a renewed sense of revelation, and that my prayers that You will intervene will come to fruition.

Thankfully, I let His grace, peace, and love wash over me, ensuring that I have the constant comfort with my Prince of Peace readily available. He has died on the cross so that I can have the unquavering knowledge that I have a new identity, because all my sins have been washed clean, as white as snow, placing me in the loving arms of the Most High.

I want to link the following scripture to my prayer:
Mark 9:23
"Then Jesus said to him, 'If you can, everything is possible to the one who believes.'"

My prayer is that the question on the way towards discerning the wonderful reality of His presence can give me the insight that I have been drawn closer to Him. I can rest in the knowledge that the Holy Spirit defines me, and everything is possible because He loves us, showering a cloud of mercy over us. He will ensure that my daily prayers, yearning for a clear answer, can constantly be a comfort to me once I am receptive in following His wisdom.

The impact of His grace
The scripture that the Holy Spirit reminds me of today is:

Romans 6:16

"Don't you realise that you became the slave of whatever you choose to obey? You can be a slave to sin, which leads to death, or you can choose to obey God, which leads to righteous living."

The realisation that His loving kindness, hope, and grace can carry us through everything that Satan tries to throw in our path is a promise that I have found in the words of the Gospel. Hope and love are two emotions that carry me through any situations that I may and have faced. He knows the gentle prodding needed to turn my face towards my destiny and identity in Him. I never underestimate the power of prayer and the choice I make to focus on the answers that God reveals to us, and I believe this should be made with the knowledge that He will direct each of our steps. There is also no condemnation in those that call upon His name. How wonderful it is to know that my prayers are already known to Him.

I pray the following scripture over my day:

Matthew 5:16–17 "No one lights a lamp and puts it under a basket, but rather on a lampstand, and it gives light for all who are in the house. In the same way, let your light shine before men, so that they may see your good works and give glory to your Father in heaven".

My prayer today is that I can know that I am fearfully and wonderfully made, in the image of God. Let us live this truth and continue to grow into the person He desires for us. There is a profound impact we can have once we love those around us the same as He does.

Thank You, Lord, that I can feel the vastness in my destiny to identify my right standing in You. I want to remain in the knowledge that no sin is greater than Your gift of redemption, showing how palpable the ability to rely on Your grace can be. My identity in You and my place in Your Kingdom can never be compared to my previous walk as a non-believer. You loved me enough that You were patient in drawing me closer to You, finding great joy in the moment I stepped into Your throne room.

Finding His mercy in the revelation of salvation
In the word today I am filled with inspiration to share from my heart:

1 Chronicles 16:23

"Sing unto the Lord, all the earth, shew forth day to day His salvation."

As I look back on my life before accepting the Lord as my Saviour, I can only stand in awe of the way everything has changed. He has been beside me all the time, with a gentle spirit and a profound guiding light. I have also found that sometimes I am on the same road as before, but my Prince of Peace is alongside me without any judgement, steering me clear of any untruths Satan brings about when my spiritual life is not where it needs to be.

The worship that pours out of my heart is based on the fact that when I remain in His presence, He will reveal His glory that can fill my soul with peace. I trust in the fact that He will continue the process that was started. To know that I am Yours is a constant source of peace as well as a place where my reassurance of my identity in You is very evident. You guide me through every season and ensure that the previous season's lesson learnt encourages me to rely on the knowledge that the Holy Spirit remains my steering light into righteousness.

I pray the following scripture to be aligned to the truth of

His word:

Deuteronomy 31:6

"So be strong and courageous! Do not be afraid and do not panic before Him. For the Lord, your God, will personally go ahead of you. He will neither fail you nor abandon you."

My prayer today is that the measure of my faith in Him to work all things together for my good will remain my anchor to His word, and that it will be more than enough to walk the journey of discovering new aspects of my Christian life. It will be a new season that His love will guide and carry me, where He senses that I need an increase in my level of trust. Let me be more aware of Your presence, because You have given me all the tools and guidance I need to walk closer to my salvation, that I can hold onto the truth of my existence and rejoice in it.

Let my direction of all my desires to be a conqueror be the sure footing my spirit yearns for. With gratitude I can have a great feeling of peace when I look back at Your love towards me, knowing with full confidence that Your purpose for me has always been to be loved beyond my understanding. Thank You that I can be in a place of praising Your glory every day. My God is exalted, and I will continue to acknowledge my Prince of Peace, finding my identity as being loved by My Redeemer. His peace is an everlasting covenant, and I am freely blessed in every situation. My salvation through repentance will be my constant song of praise.

My hope lies in Your promises to lift my head, and that my body, soul, and spirit will be immersed in Your mercy alone. I can be assured that you will wipe away all my tears, even before I cry out to You.

VICTORY

You are my Savior
Today the scripture on my heart is:
Psalm 63:7–8
"Because You are my help; I will rejoice in the shadow of your wings. I will follow close to You; Your right hand upholds me."

With this in mind, I want to not only experience Your presence in my life, but I want it to be evident to others because of my new tranquillity that forms my outlook on life. Jesus, I live abundantly because I can face everything, with the victory I can call upon as my ultimate prize. Because I praise Your name and draw closer to You, I am rooted firmly in Your foundation of forgiveness and grace. I can know without a doubt that You are my rock and Redeemer. Let Your everlasting power flow; let it be a healing touch and anchor to You, ensuring that all my chains have been broken. I meditate with the sole purpose to live in the knowledge that I am seated in Your heavenly Kingdom. With every step I take, I look to You; You give me all I need and even more than I could have ever dreamed of.

You have foregone all to win my heart back. Let my praise then be a part of my heart that connects with the admission that I can find my victory in You.

I pray the following scripture over my day:

Psalm 19:1

"The heavens declare Your glory; the sky proclaims the work of Your hands."

Today, I want to acknowledge that I will remain in a place of joy, because in times of hardships, I can rest under the shadow of Your wings. I want to find my treasure in the vast, majestic presence I search for, and find, when I sing praises of redemption, continuing to long for Your love. As the heavens declare the work of Your hands, I also want to proclaim my everlasting devotion to You. You have saved me, and once again as the thunder roars, You refresh my soul with Your cleansing river of life.

I want to declare my covenant to You without fail, and I will ensure that I am in a place where I long for Your glory to shine forever, as I rely on Your promise of everlasting life. You are my cornerstone through every storm, and I want to remain rooted in Your healing touch to flood my journey with a constant stream of grace. Let me hand over these heavy burdens, for they are not in Your plans for me. I am thankful to know that You can send your everlasting peace over my situation. I am being held up with Your right hand; I cry out for my soul to be refreshed with every moment I spend in my quiet time dwelling in Your word.

No more seasons of failures

The scripture that I want to link to the knowledge that there will be no more seasons of failures, and that I can worship Him in all His holy splendour, is the following:

1 Chronicles 16:29

"Give to the Lord the glory He deserves! Bring your

offering and come into His presence. Worship the Lord in all His holy splendor."

Many challenges have directed my path to crossroads, and once I have prayed over the specific situation, I can confidently walk towards my destiny, knowing that I can take comfort in the fact that we have victory because death has been defeated. A while ago, I spoke of the fact that the joy of the Lord is my strength, and I pray that I will continue to put my delight in Him, and in return He will give me beauty from ashes. Our Redeemer makes us new, redeemed people, and we can worship the Lord for His steadfast love and mercy. I long to worship my Redeemer, because from the moment of our salvation, God's intent with the rest of our lives on earth is that we will be changed into the image of His Son, Jesus.

I pray over my day:

Isaiah 55:11

"So is my word that goes out from my mouth: It will not return to me empty but will accomplish what I desire and achieve the purpose for which I sent it."

Let me reflect Your glory and grace, and that my worship will be from an overflow of a grateful heart. Thank you that I know that when I first believed in Jesus, there was a deep and immediate gratefulness for the unearned forgiveness of sin, the assurance of God's love, the promise of heaven, the restoration of our relationship with God. Let my faith create a boldness that ensures that my failures are no longer a part of me; there is no judgement that consumes me. I hold onto the presence of the Holy Spirit to ensure that I walk with the knowledge that I am never alone, being guided by the truths I find in the word.

HOPE

Renewed sense of amazement

The hope I find in my God of miracles, places me in the state where I find my heart is in a place of worship, filled with a renewed sense of amazement that I have a part in His wonderful Kingdom, with abundant blessings of grace and mercy, carrying me towards a battle that has already been conquered by Your power.

What this means is that I can run to You for refuge; I can have great confidence as I hold onto the hope that lies before me. Let my heart be faithful in the revelation that I can find when I am seated in the revelation that my destiny will be a constant anchor, and my strength endures to safeguard the knowledge that every moment has been enforced by Your commanding hand.

With this in mind, the scripture that the Lord has reminded me of is:

Psalm 119:74:

"Those who fear You will see me and rejoice, for I put my hope in Your word."

I will remain in the shelter that I find in You, never wavering from Your constant mercy that is poured over my spirit, without being held back.

Thank You that I can rely on the fact that You are consistent in Your graceful love that is still such a wonder. When I acknowledge that Your divine power and destiny is for me, and behind me, and upholds me, there will be no mountain or valley too high for me to defeat any strongholds over me.

I pray the following scripture over my hunger for more hope in You:

James 1:12

"Blessed is a man who endures trials, because when he passes the test, he will receive the crown of life that He has promised to those who love Him."

My prayer is that I can stand on the strong foundation to know that You are a God that never changes through the ages. The trials that I face will not take me to a place where I move without You, because the hope that I can only find in You, My Prince of Peace, guides my steps towards Your inner sanctuary.

I will lift my eyes to the Heavens above, walking with my head held high. Your love is here to stay. I can confidently state that my healing has been planned in advance, and I can walk with the knowledge that no weapon formed against me will prosper.

I believe that You saved me, even when I refused to acknowledge Your power in my life. Without You, Jesus, I am stuck in spiritual darkness; only You can rescue me in times of trouble. Sin and death were conquered for all; this we can see in the fellowship where rejoicing and songs of praise can ensure that every spirit-filled believer will pour out.

Let Your fire consume my troubles, ensuring that I rely on You alone, placing Your Kingdom before all else. I am righteous in Your eyes, and I will remain rooted to this fact. I am picking up the pieces that the storm has left behind, bringing me to a new sense of belonging. Thank You that I can find rest that is everlasting in You. I rely on Your promise that my perception of who I am in You is sure and confirmed in my most inner part.

When I ponder on what my constant life song of praise will look like to reveal Your majesty in my spirit-filled life, I will endeavour to broaden my horizon with this in mind.

BRINGING CLARITY TO THE RENEWED RIGHTEOUS STANDING I HAVE IN HIM

The scripture on my heart today is:

Habakkuk 2:14

"For the earth will be filled with the knowledge of the Lord's glory, as the waters cover the sea."

With this in mind, I have found that the invitation to bring about the trust that my faith in experiencing His everlasting love can be known in my innermost thoughts, will bring clarity to any situation. How wonderful it is to know that Jesus was sent to bring me back to the arms of the Lord!

He constantly reassures me that I can be bold in drawing close to Him in my prayers, ensuring that all my fears are taken care of. The word is clear on us taking comfort that each day is new with abundant mercies, as well assuring us that we should not concern ourselves with what tomorrow holds.

There can be seasons of thinking that Satan knows how to steal, kill, and destroy our faith, and the fear that the Lord will abandon us in the hour of need. But what a comfort it is that we are not condemned for our sins, but that we are born again by the Holy Spirit. From that moment on, there are no words to describe the revelation that any desperation I have felt is being lifted to Heaven. The language of my salvation is a balm to our Abba Father's ears, ensuring that my righteous standing is embedded in my most inner being.

I choose to remain a faithful servant and be Kingdom-focused in an effort to make a difference in a small way. I believe by doing this I can show His grace and mercy throughout my interaction with others, exposing the peace that comes when my foundation in my faith is rooted in His grace. My experience is that I can have the boldness to enter His throne room, because He has placed a clear understanding that I can declare the freedom that stems from sitting at the feet of Jesus. I do not have to feel that my difficulties are impossible to be conquered. He never expects me to do this without His guidance and reminders of His faithfulness to bring the clarity of my salvation as my ultimate prize.

There is no doubt that I need to trust that my innermost desires and dreams are already known to Him, that they will be taken care of. I can have faith that He will deal with all my needs for that specific situation on my heart.

Today my prayer is that the Lord will give me the power of inner strength so that my entire life will be built on the adoration that flows from Him. The power of Your love surrounds me with an everlasting peace I can only find in You, because I can draw closer to Your mercy. I will remain in a place of worship due to the revelation that I can conquer everything through You, and that You see every tear that I shed, considering those difficulties I endure but am afraid of giving over to you are washed away by the blood that Jesus shed for our old selves.

Thank you that you listen to my prayer from the ends of the earth, where I call out to You. When my heart is faint, You reassure me of Your grace and mercy.

Only You can satisfy my hunger to worship and rejoice in heaven's grace. Thank You that the pressure is off me to perform, that I can always find a resting place in You, My Savior. Through You, nothing is impossible. I run towards the righteousness that was spoken over me since the beginning of time.

I will find peace in the knowledge that I am not meant to be in a place of feeling out of control, as I know with full confidence that I am under the covering of Your wings.

The work of the cross

The scripture on my heart today is:

Romans 8:28–39

"And we know that in all things God works for the good of those who love him, who have been called according to his purpose. For those God foreknew he also predestined to be conformed to the image of his Son, that he might be the firstborn among many brothers and sisters. And those he predestined, he also called; those he called, he also justified; those he justified, he also glorified."

What, then, shall we say in response to these things? If God is for us, who can be against us? He who did not spare his own Son, but gave him up for us all — how will he not also, along with him, graciously give us all things? Who will bring any charge against those whom God has chosen? It is God who justifies. Who then is the one who condemns? No one other than Satan. Christ Jesus who died — more than that, who was raised to life — is at the right hand of God and is also interceding for us. Who shall separate us from the love of Christ? Shall trouble or hardship or persecution or famine or nakedness or danger or sword? As it is written in Psalm 44:22:

"For your sake we face death all day long;
we are considered as sheep to be slaughtered."

Another scripture I want to highlight is found in Romans 8:26–39: "No, in all these things we are more than conquerors through him who loved us. For I am convinced that neither death nor life, neither angels nor demons, neither the present nor the future, nor any powers, neither height nor depth, nor anything else in all creation, will be able to separate us from the love of God that is in Christ Jesus our Lord.

Upon reflecting on this scripture, I had a sense that the work of the cross means that He went through suffering as a man but was raised up as the only living Son. I am favoured and blessed because of this; I am born again, with no sin evident due to the greatest forgiveness of God. I also had a sense that the joy set before us has always been the Father's plan to send Jesus, for us to be adopted as His children, ensuring that a relationship with us is evident in the way we respond to His word.

He makes us holy and justified. We can carry the glory of His character; all we have to do is cooperate. We are not just soldiers in His army; we are called to a destiny of greatness. How wonderful it is to know that Jesus is our older brother.

My prayer is that I will continue to proclaim Your hand in my spiritual walk, and that my heart will echo with the promise that neither death nor life, neither angels nor demons, neither the present nor the future, nor any powers, neither height nor depth, nor anything else in all creation, will be able to separate me from the love of God that is in Christ Jesus our Lord. I call upon Jesus to be victorious through Him that pours out adoration towards me, unrestricted, never-ending, and lasting through every storm.

You are high and lifted and Your Kingdom has no end. Your love is still such a wonder; Your cross still brings me to my knees. Because Your grace draws me closer to my destiny, I find myself in Your inner sanctuary, bringing forth a refuge from the world, and the fellowship I have with my Counsellor will calm my heart. I want to proclaim from the depth of my soul that I will not let my heart be like wax, melting within me.

I pray the following scripture over my heart and spirit today:
Psalm 139:15–16
"My bones were not hidden from You when I was made in secret, when I was formed in the depths of the earth. Your eyes saw me when I was formless, all my days were written in Your book and planned before a single one of them began."
It is a revelation to know how much God loves me; it comes out of love, protection. His love is poured out with abundance; there is a God that places before me concrete rules to protect me from the world around us that should not continue to speak untruths over us.

While I remained in a place of rejecting Your wonderful presence, You still continued to love and protect me. There is a higher way that You watch over me, freely giving me the opportunity to take cover under Your calming presence. This reflects Your character of grace and mercy; I am a child of the Prince of Peace, King of the nations.

You are strong to save
The scripture on my heart today is:
Micah 7:7–8.
"But as for me, I watch in hope for the Lord, I wait for God my Saviour; my God will hear me. Do not gloat over me,

my enemy! Though I have fallen, I will rise.
Though I sit in darkness, the Lord will be my light."

I am thankful because when I am at my worst, held captive by my sins and rebelling against You, Jesus will intervene and bring back peace, magnificence, and mercy. I will keep on worshipping You, Lord, that no matter how dark my day is, You are still God, and You remain faithful to Your promises.

Knowing this changes my perspective and ensures that I can be in righteous standing in Your eternal light.

My prayer today is that You are the King of creation, placing each one of us at the feet of Jesus. You loved us unconditionally and sacrificed everything to be victorious in the life that was created since the beginning of Your Kingdom. No amount of darkness can steal away the radiant light that You bring about. I can walk through any fire without fear. There is a river of refuge, a calming outpouring of shelter, a holding place where I can enter into without judgment; it overspills with the power of the Holy Spirit, my Almighty God that conquers every part of my soul.

I want to thank You, continually, as You protect me from any danger this world tries to make me lose my way into Your light. I want to remain in Your light and be amazed into a glorious identity that I am living in peace and hope, giving me beauty for my ashes.

My prayer today is that even when I walk in the shadow of darkness, Your perfect love has been casting out all my fears. I will dwell in Your temple, and I praise You with an anthem of love that will glorify, bless, and honour Your name. Nothing soothes me as much as the balm of Your words of wisdom and comfort.

The confidence I find in the boldness of my faith will be the melody of adoration in my heart, shouting out loud that You are the Lord of the universe. I want to wait to become more rooted in the strength that comes from You alone. I am thankful, because You have never let go of me, through the calm and through the storm. I will focus on the revelation of Your forgiveness to make me strong in my faith and a prayerful journey that will bring me to a new understanding of reverence.

Standing on Your truth

The scripture on my heart today is:

Micah 7:7–8

"But as for me, I watch in hope for the LORD, I wait for God my Saviour; my God will hear me. Do not gloat over me, my enemy! Though I have fallen, I will rise.

Though I sit in darkness, the LORD will be my light."

Thank you that I can dwell under Your wings, because when I am at my worst, held captive by my sins and rebelling against You, Jesus intervenes and brings back peace, majesty, and mercy. Thank You, Lord, that no matter how dark my day is, You are still God, and You remain good.

Knowing this changes my perspective and ensures that I can be in righteous standing in Your eternal light. No amount of darkness can steal away the radiant light that You bring about. I can walk through any fire without fear. There is a river of refuge, a holding place where I can enter without judgment; it overflows with the power of the Holy Spirit.

Even when I walk in the shadow of darkness, I need to rely on Your perfect love to cast out all my fears. I will dwell in Your temple, and I praise You with the goal to glorify, bless and honor Your name. Nothing soothes me as much as the balm of Your words of wisdom and comfort. The confidence I find in the boldness of my faith will be the anthem in my heart, shouting out loud that You are the Lord of the universe. I want to wait to become more rooted in the strength that comes from You alone. I am in a place of worship because You have never let go of me, through the calm and through the storm.

Your desire for me is to make me strong, creating in me a spiritual awakening. I want to acknowledge that when I define where my weaknesses stem from, I can rely on the fact that I can attempt to live in Your holy place of forgiveness, showing the majesty of Your hand in my journey of fellowship.

Because You are my fortress, I will continue to take a moment to reflect on how You have changed my life. I want to follow Your gentle prompting that I should live in the place of worship in order to bring a sense of hope and freedom to my soul.

My prayer today is that You are the King of creation, placing each one of us at the feet of Jesus. You loved us unconditionally and sacrificed everything to be victorious in the life that was created since the beginning of Your Kingdom.

You have perfect insight into my life, bringing about my deliverance. Let my life song sing, making my spirit soar to new heights. You are my stronghold, fulfilling my vows, day by day. You are who You are, finding me wherever I am.

My prayer today is that I want to thank You, always, for protecting me from any danger this world tries to make me lose my way into your light. I want to live in your light and be amazed into living.

My prayer today is that even when I walk in the shadow of darkness, that Your perfect love has been casting out all my fears. I will dwell in Your temple, and I praise You with the goal to glorify, bless, and honor Your name. Nothing soothes me as much as the balm of Your words of wisdom and comfort. The confidence I find in the boldness of my faith will be the anthem in my heart, shouting out loud that You are the Lord of the universe. I want to wait to become more rooted in the strength that comes from You alone. I am in a place of worship because You have never let go of me, through the calm and through the storm.

I pray the following scripture over my life today:

Psalm 66:19–20

"But God has surely listened and has heard my prayer.

Praise be to God, who has not rejected my prayer, or withheld His love from me."

Thank You that I no longer run in the wrong direction. You place before me blessings, so that I can be a daughter of the most High. Remind me that when I am carried away by the busyness of this world, I do not have the wrong conception that I am in place of weakness.

Finding reassurance in the promise of Salvation

The scripture on my heart today is:

Psalm 32:5

"My shield is with God who saves the upright in love. God is a righteous God, judge and a God who executes justice every day."

I can be reassured in the promise that God has made, because He has treated me generously. My heart is glad, and my spirit rejoices; my body also rests securely. Thank You that my cry for help has reached Your ears. When great floodwaters come my way, they will not reach me. I do not have to stand on a stronghold of fear. You are my help and shield; You are my Redeemer, my Prince of Peace and Counsellor.

Let hope arise in me; let me find reassurance that I can be surrounded by Your unconditional love. You are everything to me. I give thanks, because all I have is available once I proclaim Your majesty.

My prayer today is that my praise will overflow from a place of security and that my identity can be found in Your throne room.

Because I acknowledge Your rightful place in my life, my face is radiant with joy; I will never again feel ashamed. Your angels encamp around me, because I fear nothing, You rescue me from the deepest sea. Your love is bigger than the galaxies; the wonder I place in You renews my spirit every day.

You ask me to place Your Kingdom first, and all my blessings will be granted; my heart pours out my praise. Because You are my King and Saviour, I can proclaim Your majestic miracles as my own. Because I know Your name and trust in You, You have not abandoned me, because I seek Your face in all that I do. No other name is above Yours; in the times of trouble You lift me up into Your loving embrace.

I stand on Your promises of eternal life. I can have an abundant life; I can have the confidence to believe for even more power in my Christian walk of faith. Thank You that I can run towards You and find my refuge in You.

I will know without a doubt that I can walk on water, placing my complete faith, trust and sense of peace before You. Lord, take my hand and make my spirit aware of the comfort and guarantee of my salvation.

I will think of You with precious thoughts. You are the light for eternity, and I will not move without You. When I proclaim that Jesus is the Lord of my life, show me where I can find areas of emptiness; let my faith be strengthened.

I pray the following scripture over my spirit today:

Psalm 32:3–5

"When I kept silent, my bones wasted away through my groaning all day long.

For day and night Your hand was heavy on me; my strength was sapped as in the heat of summer. Then I acknowledged my sin to You and did not cover up my iniquity. I said, 'I will confess my transgressions to the LORD.' And You forgave the guilt of my sin."

I also pray with a thankful heart to press through any situation, because You alone craft my heart, drawing me closer to Your grace. When I embrace Your love, it is done not with my head but with my heart. My heart has a home, and it is not in a place but a Person, who will never let go, and that is You, my Prince of Peace, the Lord of my life.

The flawless words of the Gospel

The scripture on my heart today is the following:

Psalm 12:6–7

"And the word of the Lord is flawless, like silver purified in a crucible, like gold refined seven times. You, Lord, will keep the needy safe and will protect us forever from the wicked."

I can proclaim that being rooted in Your promises is a wonderful revelation, especially today. I will not be ashamed to declare that You are my solid foundation of righteousness.

My place in this world cannot compare to the one You have promised me, and I can remain in this season because

You are a faithful God. My place in Your Kingdom will be my reward, because Your love for me is based on the work of the cross, placing before me the ultimate prize of eternal life. You have never disappointed me, because I rely on the fact that my trust in You turns my sorrow into joy. You guide my life; I will pursue and obey Your commands. I serve the God of second chances, because You have promised me that those whose hands and hearts are pure never tell lies and never worship idols.

I do not have to feel forsaken, because You have loved me first, creating me in Your image. Thank You, Lord, that I find You when I need You most. Let me be in a place of worship during the storms of this world. I will endure these for a brief period that You can turn around for a season of joy and dancing. My heart still beats with the realization that the importance of my first encounter with You, my Lord, King and Saviour, cannot be taken away from me. I have the assurance that the worst suffering will be made bearable, because I know that You are by my side and Your grace will carry me. Not only are You the supplier of blessings but my multiplier too. I will press on toward all You have for me.

I pray the following scripture to be in alignment with my destiny:

Isaiah 30:15

"In repentance and rest is your salvation, in quietness and trust is your strength."

My prayer today is that the above prompting of the Holy Spirit will be my anthem song. My strength is renewed each day, creating in me a pure heart and solid foundation of eternal life.

I will shift my gaze from what I see to who I know, and

that is You, my Prince of Peace. Due to Your hand in my life, I can grow into maturity. I can change and grow into a new creation; I will not let anything stand in the way of the precious destiny You have for me.

I will be thankful that You brought me into a river of transformation; I am no longer lost in the fire I had to endure. You have brought me to a place of abundance. I am lost without You; You alone are my Rock of Shelter, giving me the right to call upon Your name.

Growing into maturity

In my present moment of adoration, the following scripture has taken root in my soul:

Psalm 27:1

"The Lord is my light and my salvation, so why should I be afraid? The Lord is my fortress protecting me from danger, so why should I tremble."

I am constantly aware that I can be a part of Your Kingdom just as I am. God can do way more with my surrendered heart than I can with my wrongful knowledge that I am in control of my situation. I am in a place of peace, because I am not devoid of hope, and I am engaged in a wonderful relationship with my Rock and Redeemer. My fellowship ensures that I am confident in my walk as a believer.

I want to rely on the promise that I am Yours and I have been called by Your name as a rightful, victorious child of God. No amount of darkness can steal away the radiant light that You bring about. I can walk through any fire without fear. If there is anything unclean in my spirit, let me bring my shaking heart before Your throne room. You have promised me that You are the God of calming waters; You speak the truth of the Gospel over me.

I believe that my identity and destiny have already been granted to me; let me remain in a place of worship during my time of distress.

Let me understand that somehow my heart believes without any doubts that You see me in a light of righteousness. Tomorrow holds my dreams, but today I am on my knees, looking up into the journey of grace, serving You into eternity. The fruits and the gifts of the Spirit can turn my ordinary existence into a new creation. You lead me to the highest place of worthiness; everything my heart desires is mine, because I place my delight in You.

If I turn back time, it will not bring forth a sense of shame, because my sins cannot overwhelm my spirit. Any amount of shame will be crushed as the memories in between my salvation and today mean that I can proclaim the priority that my spiritual walk must remain at. My heart finds a home as I declare Your majestic grace in my spirit; at the forefront of my prayers is only You.

I can grow into maturity with Your mercy as my ultimate prize; what was meant for harm will raise me up from my past mistakes.

I pray the following scripture over my day:
Isaiah 25:1
"I will honor You and praise Your name. You have done amazing things; You have faithfully carried out the plans You made long ago."

My prayer today is that I will remain in the place of gratefulness that I can live in a place of shelter, ensuring that my complete surrender brings about the victory that is mine.

You are my light and salvation; I can step out of darkness, because You have overcome the cross and the grave is empty. You have passed through death and turned into resurrection.

Death is not a part of Your being. I choose not to remain in a place where I broke Your heart, I close my eyes in wonder, because You adore me and rejoice in the words of my prayer. They are from the deepest depths of my soul. I want to take one more step with Your hand lifting me up towards heaven's embrace. I hold onto Your strength, and You remind me that if I take the control that binds my soul out of my own hands, I can live the resurrected life You have planned for me.

A God of restoration

I pray the following scripture over my day:

Isaiah 54:10

"'Though the mountains be shaken, and the hills be removed, yet my unfailing love for you will not be shaken nor my covenant of peace be removed,' says the LORD, who has compassion on you."

I will ensure that I am prepared for Your return. I will persist to be in a place where You influence every part of my being. I was wasting time, to rely on somebody to love me with worldly love, but You entered my life and loved me with an unfailing love. I adore You because of this.

You have promised me a seat in Your throne room, where I can find a sense of freedom that forms a bedrock, with my sure footing in Your Kingdom.

I am Your faithful servant; You know my heart and deepest desires. You complete each of Your many promises; You turn my problems around so that they convert into abundant promises. You are true to Your word; no name is higher than Yours. I can rely on the fact that the time that I dwell in Your presence is pleasing to my Saviour's eyes. Thank you that I am not marked by my disabilities, but You see me as righteous.

Everywhere I go, Your hands uplift me while the hills shake; You are my wonderful Counsellor. What You see in me is more than enough; to have a part in Your Kingdom, my whole being is being swept under the covering of Your wings, and I can continually hear the whispering words of Your reassurance that You will never leave my side. Anything I deem as broken, that holds me back from my destiny, has been mended by Your mercy. God, You bring order, making me whole.

My prayer is that it will never be too late to acknowledge the importance of Your covenant with me. Thank you that You have chosen me before the beginning of time. You enable me to live with hope in my heart, because I know that my suffering in this life will eventually result in eternal glory. I have a Father that promises me that His grace can lift me up from any season of despair. Your promise and existence of peace remains at the heart of the openness I find in You.

I pray that the following scripture will carry me through any dark day:

Psalm 139:5–6

"You hem me in behind and before and lay Your hand upon me. Such knowledge is too wonderful for me, too lofty for me to attain."

I do not have to wonder where the abundant life for a Christ-follower is; joy and victory shines a light into my journey as a daughter of the most High.

Though this world of uncertainty shakes, my love for You will not quiver. Let Your mercy rain. Thank You that You break the cycle of unbelief. I will shout Your name from every possible mountain. Thank You that You have converted my heart into a new one, ensuring that I can walk with my head held high.

You are my God of restoration. While I make the decision to place Your kingdom first, all other priorities fall away. My wrongful thinking of the previous sins that held me back is covered by Your grace.

God of revealing His floodwaters

The scripture on my heart today is:

Psalm 29:10–11

"The Lord rules over the floodwaters. The Lord reigns as King forever. The Lord gives his people strength. The Lord blesses them with peace."

With this revelation, I am thankful. Because of Your continually blessings, Lord, You come to my rescue. I do not have to wait in despair during my time of feeling forsaken. Let fear be far from my heart; let Your comforting presence drain away any tribulations.

Every area of my being, and all I ever have to be, has already been spoken over me.

I have the revelation that for the first time, I can rely on Your strength, as I am unique, truly loved, cherished and a most precious daughter of Your glorious Kingdom. I will be just at Your feet, on my knees, as I acknowledge my salvation. As long as I have the ability to declare Your power in my life, I will not miss another minute of praising Your name.

I will believe that the heavens will pour out abundant blessings. I want to be a beautiful shady place, to give other believers a soft landing, as they perceive Your hand in my life, as I marvel in the love and grace that surrounds me.

I do not have to walk in in a world where my past consumes my spirit, as You give me a pure and clean heart. My strength is a sure promise, followed by a sense of peace and believing that Your grace remains my ever-present shield of favour, where I can stand on Your promises of unconditional love, where my adoration can flow freely. As the ends of the earth worship Your name, I will persevere to take hold of the sure footing of grace. Since I live in the Spirit, I will keep in step with the Spirit.

I want to dwell under the protection of Your wings, as my worship is a weapon and shield to remove any season of darkness in my walk with You, Lord, my Saviour. Your love lifts me up towards my destiny of a faith-filled life, guiding me into persistent moments of victory. The love I found in You has guided all my steps. I do not have to live in a place of trouble, because You are by my side, always whispering words of comfort, guiding me in the knowledge that You are ever present.

Your word promises me that I will see the light, as I continue to be the one that holds on, and that is a wonderful miracle to perceive that renews my soul.

My prayer today is that because there is a cloud of grace, I can remain rooted in the realization that my soul acknowledges that it must be an undying devotion to You, my Prince of Peace. As You rule over the floodwaters in my life, I see that Your healing rain nourishes the void of anguish in me. I will never fail to lose sight of the victory that is mine. The previous foundation of my life where I was feeling despondent has been replaced by an anthem of overcoming my seasons of obscurity. Thank you that Your blessing of peace covers my heart with overflowing awe of Your wonderful grace, even though You found me struggling to hear and heed Your voice.

I also want to reveal the desires of my heart that You will remind me that storms will come, and storms will go, but I do not have to tremble in fear, as You are my solid foundation, my Lord of Light. Thank You that the extent of all my dreams will satisfy my heart, and that I will meditate on the promises of victory. I do not have to perform to receive every blessing, because I have access to take ownership of these blessings.

I pray that the message in John 20:31 will define the true meaning of my walk of Your divine power:

"But these are written that You may believe that Jesus is the Christ, the son of God, and that by believing You may have life in His name."

You are the God of wonders and triumph, everlasting King and Counsellor, watching over me. My devotion is complete; my soul rejoices with a song, praising Your holy name, Abba Father and Comforter of my heart. Seeking intimacy with You will manifest Your power in transforming my innermost being.

A shield of worship
The scripture that found a place in my heart today is:
John 1:9

"If we confess our sins; He is faithful and just and will forgive our sins and purify us from all unrighteousness."

In a place of revelation with this true word in mind, I pray that my worship will be a shield and weapon to remove any time of darkness in my passage and fellowship with You, Lord, My Saviour. I believe that it can be difficult to walk on the waves of blessings and promises of prosperity that restore our souls, but acknowledging our Counsellor and Comforter will draw us closer to where He wants us to find a resting place.

I can be the creation You have intended me to be, as I am unique and genuinely loved with a tenderness. Let my heart rejoice while I ponder on the revelation that I am cherished, adored like no other, and a most precious daughter of His Glorious Kingdom. You see it through to the end. I believe that You have never failed me; You have released me from the darkness and despair. I do not have to fear, because when I am in a place where I dwell on untruths where I feel forsaken, You will run to my rescue.

I trust You to steer me towards a glowing promise of safe shores. You are closer than a whisper, journeying by my side towards the road to redemption. You alone are my salvation. You alone are my Redeemer and Miracle maker.

Let Your fire fall again, as I pray to be aware that the gentle prompting at this moment can result in me being reminded that storms will come, and they will go. I do not have to despair or remain rooted to a foundation of abandonment, because You are my Rock, Redeemer, and God of Restoration.

All my dreams will fill my heart, and I will constantly meditate on the confirmation that I am alive to live the dreams that have found me in a season of rejoicing. Remind me that I can find secure footing in the establishment of Jesus Christ, as He was sent from our Heavenly Father to let grace and truth guide us to reclamation. I want to walk in awestruck wonder at the mention of Your name; no name is above Your name. You reveal Your character to change my perception of my life before I acknowledged the majesty of Your Kingdom. I am a new creation, destined to have freedom to raise me higher than ever before, where I will shout from the rooftops that You alone fill my soul with a life song of joy.

Thank you that I can live in the wonderful place where You are my only identity-gatekeeper. I can feel You move my mountains to be shaken in order for me to see the battle that is Yours. Your arm of love draws me near to Your mercy and grace, bringing amazement of Your wonder to every step I am able to take.

Let me remain on my knees in my rightful place in Your throne room. I can be all you created me to be in order to broaden the everlasting revelation that victory is for those that hold onto Your desires for us to be more than conquerors. I will declare that a new season of hope and joy is readily available for the one that places all their delight in You.

Displaying the wonders available within our reach
The scripture that has brought me to full revelation of my rightful standing in Your Kingdom is the following:

Psalm 17:7

"Display the wonders of Your faithful love, Saviour of all who seek refuge from those who rebel against Your right hand."

With this in mind, I have been blessed with the revelation that Your splendour is seen in all through the majestic world we live in, and through Your everlasting love I can be assured that You are right beside me during all my experiences as a refreshed, new creation. Before I try to fathom the extent of Your love, make me more aware of my destiny and identity in You. As you daily recreate me, all I have to do is to be obedient to the prompting of the Holy Spirit.

I can shout with joy because of the revelations I have been privileged to remain a daughter of the King of all creation.

Every time I feel a need to seek comfort in Your word, I find it, and it is revealed in so many different ways, and this makes me believe with everything in my soul that eternal life with You is going to be a great, wonderful, and amazing seasons. You have rebuilt so many aspects of my life, and my love for You is stronger than ever before. I believe that the fellowship I find in You will be a firm affirmation that the best is yet to come.

The life You have spoken over me releases promises that will bring about a song of praise, lifting me higher towards heaven. I pray that You will remind me to open my spiritual eyes, because You have loved me with an unconditional, undying love. The only action You ask of me is to place Your Kingdom first. You are the hand that leads me home; let fear be far from my heart.

I pray that You will turn my mourning into joy and continue to live with the knowledge that I do not have to conform to previous notions of being weighed down for the sins that Jesus has died and delivered me from. Your power is a stronghold for the growth and renewal of my faith, as well as an everlasting pledge of obedience.

I pray Hebrews 13:15 over this moment of my life:

"Through Jesus Christ, let us continually offer to God a sacrifice of praise, the fruit of lips that openly profess His name."

I live in the knowledge that You are my Saviour. All who seek refuge from those who rebel against Your right hand will be raised up into eternal joy, with a gentle prompting by the Holy Spirit that guides me towards my righteousness.

HIS HEALING

Experiencing the fullness of God

There is a very well-known gospel song whereby the chorus has the following line "He gives and takes away, my heart will choose to say, Blessed be His name!" The song is "Blessed Be Your Name" by Matt Redman.

It was not clear in my understanding, that these two actions within one sentence, could be grouped together. My previous experience has been of a God that blesses us, showers us with love, grace, mercy, and favor like no other. Removing or taking away in the context of being a child of God had not ever crossed my thoughts, but this now has a new meaning, as I have listened to the prompting of His whisper.

Upon reflection, I can now see that the Lord has taken away from me the questions, the sadness, and the complete state of internal turmoil that was a part of me, because these are not in my destiny as a victorious servant of God. Without the assurance from our Heavenly Father's covering and presence, I cannot make decisions that are not according to His will. We can often find ourselves to be present in the moment but not taking into consideration the anointed place where His leading takes us. Someone once explained this concept as "To know if you are lost, you first have to know where you are at that exact moment."

Taking the next step in your journey towards the fullness

that His power brings cannot be stolen away by anyone, even by Satan. If you are aware of the place He wants you to be rooted in, you can find rest for your soul. Be aware of His everlasting, all consuming, unconditional love, and that it should be a choice to draw near to Him, bringing peace over any situation.

I want to speak the truth and impact the following scripture has had on me:

Jeremiah 10:12–13

"He made the earth by His power, established the world by His wisdom and spread the heavens by His understanding. When He thunders, the water in the heavens are in turmoil, and He causes the clouds to rise from the ends of the earth."

My prayer is that I will continually rely on the promises that He has been there, and always will be, in my season of darkness! There is nothing that He hides from us. Thank you, Lord, for all You are in my life, and for the freedom I find in the knowledge that I am no longer broken-hearted. I will always ask for Your healing touch, relying on the revelation that I can always find comfort in You.

Proclaim His hand in your healing

Being unashamed of being a child of God in front of others is something that I cherish every day. It is an everlasting, life-changing, peace-filled experience. God is bigger than anything Satan tries to derail you from; call upon His name, and your request will be answered. Finding rest for your soul because you can experience His hand in your healing can be a constant comfort through every season.

I also feel that the Holy Spirit is prompting me lately that my belief should be strong, and that my spiritual eyes need to be open, and my heart and soul should be receptive to the Holy Spirit to lead me into the way forward. The way my previous priorities and outlook on life dictated every day, and the change of my priorities now, will always be a reminder of the amazing moment when I chose Him above everything else.

We have the assurance that a method and solution to all questions and concerns is available, and that is prayer and the close relationship with the Holy Trinity that calms every storm. He calls us to be humble, never forgetting that seeking the Kingdom above all else is a vital part of living free and in His eyes perfect, righteous, and with a clear destiny. And the most important destiny for me is the promise of eternal life. Nothing can compare to that!

Remember that you are chosen, beautiful, anointed, and have a destiny that will amaze you. He will ensure that your life overflows with love, peace, and joy.

The scripture that I want to share on the above is:

Mark 5:33

"Then the frightened woman, trembling at the realization of what had happened to her, came and fell to her knees in front of Him and told Him what she had done."

I pray today that I will continue to acknowledge His healing power. I can be authentic, constantly molded by Him, and His Spirit in me must affect what I think, choose and feel. Being mature in faith, with Christ, comes over time, and once you realize this, the Lord will continue to urge you to extend His Kingdom. I pray that my life and the way I live my faith out should be visible in the fruit my Christian life produces.

<u>Season of healing</u>
I have walked a road of healing for a long period, and I feel

that the Lord has led me into a guiding spirit to proclaim that anyone seeking health in any area finds peace at the feet of Jesus. It can be spiritual and physical healing, or both, and in my experience, I realised that my physical condition needs to be given over to the Lord before He can minister to my spirit. A close relationship ensures that His peace guiding your way forward can pull you through any claim that Satan wants you to believe.

The scripture on my heart today is:

Psalm 143:8

"Let me hear of Your unfailing love each morning, for I am trusting You. Show me where to walk, for I give myself to You."

I pray that your walk and this close relationship will continue to be found in the unspoken desires of your prayers that the Lord is already aware of. Thanking Him is a sure recipe we can follow in order to acknowledge that when we are receptive of the Holy Spirit, He will show us where to walk, for we can freely give ourselves to Him. When I deepen my faith to align with Your promises, I can live in a place of victory. I can rely on the understanding that everything works out for those that wait for His perfect timing to guide us towards His majestic throne room, with the realization that He has healed the deepest part of us. His blood covers any area that needs restoration, without any judgement.

Filling my soul to overflow with praise

Today, my heart is reminded to recognize the following scripture to speak the truth on the importance of Your divine direction:

Psalm 32:8

"I will instruct you and teach you in the way you should go, I will counsel you with my eye upon you."

I will follow Your direction on Your Word to replenish my soul with everlasting comfort, because Your eye is upon me. I can be dependent on Your strength and lean on You to walk beside me. My heart rejoices as I am reminded of the wonderful blessings being a child of my Living God manifest over me, casting out anything that is not from You. How can I say enough how amazing is Your love, how can I not sing my praises to be heard? It fills my spirit with joy and understanding of Your everlasting grace. Your Word is the final answer. You fight the many battles for me, so that I can rely on You, without hesitation, living in perfect harmony with the ability to expand Your Kingdom.

I would like to remain in a place of worship with the following scripture:

Psalm 95:1–3

"Come, let us sing to the Lord! Let us shout joyfully to the Rock of our salvation. Let us come to Him with thanksgiving. Let us sing psalms of praise to Him. For the Lord is a great God. A great King above all gods."

My prayer is that I will see every moment of comfort that You represent in my life and let me choose to honour Your name, because the victory is already mine. Thank You, Lord, that I have found my place in Your Kingdom, so that I can have a renewed awareness in my confidence that no obstacle in my path is too big to overwhelm me. Let me fit my entire life to remain in You; let Your unfailing love surround me.

The joy of You, my Emmanuel, is my strength, and I will sing your praises because You are my Rock of salvation. When I feel that I might have been hurt, I can testify that I am not held back by this. I will glorify Your name with never-ending, continuous prayer, expanding and reaffirming my commitment in living a faith-filled life. Let me radiate Your love and grace, because it has raised me up into heaven's embrace. I will continue to marvel in Your mercy, promising me that the prophecy that Your constant healing has already been spoken over my life has taken place.

I want to acknowledge that this creation has been birthed because I obeyed a guiding whisper to ensure that I am in a place of obedience throughout the journey of sharing my testimony with others.

I want to give all the glory to Him. My prayer is that His radiant light of redemption will remain my anthem song. I will continue to walk beside Him and focus on bringing the Gospel to all.

I pray Corinthians 3:14–18 as a summary of His healing covenant and redemption that has been spoken over me.

"But the people's minds were hardened, and to this day whenever the old covenant is being read, the same veil covers their minds so that they cannot understand the truth. And this veil can be removed only by believing in Christ.

Yes, even today when they read Moses' writings, their hearts are covered with that veil, and they do not understand.

But whenever someone turns to the Lord, the veil is taken away.

For the Lord is the Spirit, and whenever the Spirit of the Lord is, there is freedom.

So all of us who have had the veil removed can see and reflect the glory of the Lord. And the Lord — who is the Spirit — makes us more like Him as we are changed into His glorious image."

My dream that the Lord has placed on my heart is that I am thankful, because He has spoken over me the prophecy that I should rely on my spiritual eyes and ears, because I listened to the prompting to turn towards the Lord. Jesus is a worthy sacrifice, and I accept Him as my King and Saviour. I will fight the good fight of faith and take hold of my eternal life to which I was called when I made my good confession in the presence

of many witnesses.

Thank You, Abba Father, that I have the boldness that comes from the freedom I find in You to reflect Your mercy and glory in the foundation of my journey, to inspire anyone that needs understanding in the redemption that comes through consistent prayer and remaining rooted in the truth of the Gospel. Thank You that I refused to allow Satan's work to corrode my life and soul. I can live in a place of worship, because my character is not compromised throughout times of darkness.

Thank You that I am seated at the feet of Jesus, acknowledging the salvation that has been granted to me, freely, without any judgement.

I will revive the promise that to be rooted to the affirmation of my identity in Christ is a sure way to enter into His throne room. Christ lives in me, completing His covering of unconditional, everlasting love. There is nothing that can steal this away from me, as You guide me to pray in earnest and trust that my faith is a pleasing sight in Your eyes.